FAST FORWARD

New Saskatchewan Poets

edited by

BARBARA KLAR & PAUL WILSON

HAGIOS
PRESS

Copyright © 2007 Hagios Press

Library and Archives Canada Cataloguing in Publication

Fast forward : new Saskatchewan poets / edited by Barbara Klar & Paul Wilson.

ISBN 0-9739727-5-0

1. Canadian poetry (English) – Saskatchewan. 2. Canadian poetry (English) – 21st century. I. Klar, Barbara, 1966- II. Wilson, Paul, 1954-

PS8295.5.S3F38 2007   C811'.608097124   C2007-901824-6

Designed and typeset by Donald Ward.
Cover art: *The South Wind* by Terry Fenton (used with permission of the artist).
Cover design by Yves Noblet.
Set in Goudy Oldstyle, titles in Trajan Pro.
Printed and bound in Canada at Houghton Boston Printers & Lithographers, Saskatoon.

The publishers gratefully acknowledge the assistance of the Saskatchewan Arts Board, The Canada Council for the Arts, and the Cultural Industries Development Fund (Saskatchewan Department of Culture, Youth & Recreation) in the production of this book.

Contents

Afterwords

FOREWORD

Saskatchewan is shaped like a big empty page. The blank page, the Chinese say, contains the infinite. There are infinite ways for snow to fall; there are infinite ways for the poem to be written.

It's been a generation since the publication of the last anthology of new Saskatchewan poets. Almost overnight, it seems, another group of poets has surfaced in the community and grabbed the attention of the literary journals. It is time to showcase them, to gather their voices and celebrate a changing consciousness. Six hundred pages of submissions later, *Fast Forward* is the result.

While a few of these poems are about place, an anthology of Saskatchewan poets is not necessarily about being here. Poetry is by definition innovation; each of these poets has turned a unique form of experience into art. These poets are looking up from the prairies toward possibility and a broad world view with subjects as diverse as ancestry, love, birth, death, history, nature, and growing old.

A word on our vision: we wanted *Fast Forward* to represent a wide sphere of new poets rather than just the younger generation, so we did not impose an age limit. The poets range from their early 20s to their 60s. For some, this anthology represents their first major publication; others are nearing the completion of their second books. More women than men submitted to the anthology, and most submissions were from poets in urban centres rather than rural ones. The work we chose echoes these imbalances. We also wanted the anthology to reflect a sense of freshness, so we solicited only unpublished work. None of these poems has appeared in print before. And, as the anthology evolved, we decided to solicit essays from several of the poets as a way of complementing the poems and exploring the thinking behind them. *Fast Forward* affirms that not only is poetry alive and well in Saskatchewan, but there is a lively and cogent discussion happening here on poetics and craft. "Afterwords" is another type of snow, another river leading to the infinite.

Here are twenty-seven poets whose books we're sure you'll be reading in the decades to come. We hope you enjoy discovering them as much as we did.

Barbara Klar & Paul Wilson
March 2007

THE POEMS

October Light

1.

Not the flute-song light of April,
of skittish creek waves or
the heart-in-throat jitter
of aspen leaves.

2.

When you peel the husk back.

3.

Allspice, cinnamon, unwashed hair,
cloves pinned to over-ripe oranges,
sweat of yesterday's labour.

4.

Doesn't turn around though it can feel the eyes at its back.

5.

Not November's slag-light, the thing said
by a lover that cannot be taken back and now sits
between them broken-winged and awkward.
Not light of the thin-cough after.

6.

Inward light —
viscous magma, lamp in a night window,
light of a thought you can't yet say, blood, embers
through the seams of an old wood-stove. Light that invites,
go deeper.

7.

A thick-tongued drunken prophet, light
that spills long-shadows at your feet as if to slur.
It knows how to come to grips with the darkness
that is coming, but it's not going to say.

Bird-Bones

Air screamed through your bird-bones as you flew
from your snowmobile, into a field of snow and stubble,

once an inland sea. Your spine unhinged.
I stand around the corner of your hospital room,

Andrew, listen to my father sing as he holds your quivering legs.
What emerges from our bodies cracked open? The stiff door

of an abandoned farmhouse: orbit of dust,
flurry of dark wings. Propelled

by the thrum of your heart you landed
in a prairie of frozen stars, my father's song —

the one he sang to me when I fell here, heart-first
and screaming, into the sudden rush of sky.

That Song That Goes

      For no reason I can name
I look away from the book and see
the moon deepen into golds and reds.
Eastern sky a sodden blue. Spring
dusk is something to breathe deeply —
wet dirt, stubble, last year's leaves.
And like a dream that comes back
only when unasked for, I recall
his hands from when I was a child —
rough wood, tobacco, metal of earth.
A friend tells me of early grey mornings
at his kitchen table. There was tea,
the beginnings of a wood-fire, his wife,
bread. And the winter river-bed, the long,
slow ache I carry inside, briefly fills
with the singing of Spring melt.
Memory is that song the heart hums
along with. The one without
thinking, beneath breath.

Pierce

The woman who pierces
flesh for a living snaps
blue rubber gloves
on her long, narrow hands,
arranges her instruments —
three silver needles in sealed cellophane,
scissor-handled clamp,
cotton swabs and alcohol,
antibiotic soap.
She wears no obvious expression
or jewellery — no earrings,
studded eyebrows
or tongue.

I've had everything pierced, she tells me
everything — and everything
more than once —
it's an addiction,
an adrenaline rush, a pain
that says I'm alive —
and when the holes heal,
close over —
I get pierced again.

She leans close, marks my skin,
asks which piercing
I want first.
The one that hurts the most, I tell her,
and I hold my breath until
the first needle pushes through,
and the heat rushes in
and I breathe,
breathe,
to this place
of knowing.

December: a meditation
(with thanks to Marquez)

the first angels of December
wing around corners
remember winters lost to the sun

    slow days with no fields to turn
    sharp breath in the iron air
    I carry a load in my arms
    set it down only to sleep

        my blood crawls
        cold stones content
        in the wide river

            banks twist through the earth
            curled grass mats to kneel upon
            prayer rugs cushioned with snow
            wait for my knees

                I am caught in the arms of spruce
                trapped as ice over water

                    a twig fire burns
                    quick snap of flame
                    singes my careless glove

                        my eyes lock at the snowline
                        don't see robins on grass
                        geese overhead

I cower with spruce grouse
inert
hiding

    silent wings beating
    lessons into bone

Sport Fishing at St. Brieux

The water boils with tiny pickerel,
bodies churning
in and out of St. Brieux's bowl.

Restless boats sulking in the reeds,
men stand braced with Pilsner
lifting fish that from a distance flash like dimes.

Ed Corveau is one of them,
cap a screwed on tribute
to the Montreal Canadiens.

Ed's wife has left him,
run off to the other side of town
with Luc the Banker.

Thinking of his empty house,
Ed rips the pickerel from his hook,
its mouth a torn stem.

He throws it back,
bends to watch the blue white stomach twist,
the fins like mottled petals, sinking

and he thinks of her before the wedding
on her graduation night
how he pinned an orchid to her dress.

Betrayal

The house they built together
now defies her,
paper peeling
from cracked walls,
floorboards shifting with the tugging wind.

Nights she lies alone
and sifts through sounds
she cannot name
the rising fear
that someone's there.

Room by room, she piles furniture
in windows, doorways, thin arms stiff
as branches; hiding in the kitchen —
cans stacked just inside the door —
she counts preserves by candlelight.

But sleeping here beside the stove
cannot prevent the walls from entering her dreams,
calling moist obscenities
What is it you want? she whispers
even as her children come to pack her things.

Road Maps

He folds her body in half
quarters it, accordions it,
fits it into his mind, tucked
neatly into the glove compartment
under the licence and registration.

She flings his body wide open
upon the living room carpet,
reads legends, explores routes
well-travelled, then crumples it
feet first under the coffee table.

She leaves the front door unlocked
behind her, broken key on the mat.

When he returns home, he finds
skewed evidence, forensic shreds.

Reference points lost, he carries
a compass in his breast pocket.

Navigating forward, she maps
new routes emerging on her skin.

To Mrs. Neumann, on Receiving her Mason Jars

Your first name's a blank. All I know
is your eager death three months after your husband.
And your odd, unmarried sons, I heard about them, too,
their argument out to the dumpster and back again —
trash them, keep them, trash them —
bestowing the jars on your neighbour
who passed them on to me. Not much
of an introduction, a dozen quart sealers
scribed *Imperial* or *Improved Gem* in convex flourishes.
But they assert our sisterhood, release your aproned genie
into the steam above the stove to supervise
the boil of lids, the melt of paraffin.
We know the need, Mrs. Neumann, you and I,
to pour our love like syrup into glass,
preserve it for the darkest months ahead.
To soothe with orbs of peaches, pickles
saltier than tears. Tomatoes . . . piccalilli . . .
asparagus like downward-pointing fingers of the dead.
Could the stained glass glow of jelly on a sill
dull your husband's Auschwitz memories?
Could the prickle of coriander
dissolve the wormwood in his throat?
No matter, you tried. Let us pray, Mrs. Neumann,
for the future of peace as well as fruit and vegetables.
For love ladled out like the twin halves of pears.

Coal and *La Fée Verte*

Yesterday, Vincent and Paul indulged their hygienic practices at another *Maison de Tolerance*[*] and a girl without skin was lifted from the coal after a firedamp explosion in the *Agrappe* mine. Eight years old, shoulders scarred from the sledge, the wheel-tower in flames above her, the buildings imploded, she smelled the cooked muscles of subterranean ponies as her strange red-haired saint tore his clothes, soaked them in wax and olive oil to cover her burns, then put a piece of cheese in her black mouth. He watched her eyes, the animal that looks out from the thicket of flesh, and years later would eat cadmium red and yellow ochre, trying to kill himself with colour.

In Paris, everyone was mixing drinks. Lautrec uncapped his cane and poured something into the cognac of a dancer named Yvette. The bartender strained absinthe through sugar, mingled it with water, made it rest in Vincent's glass like weather — pale fog of lemon-emerald, *la fée verte*, poison of foxgloves (digitalis) and wormwood, the plant that grew from the path of the serpent when he slithered without legs for the first time.

And the coal-dust that settled on the grass of the Borinage like dew, the crunch underfoot of acres of embers. Vincent could have drawn using coal alone, burnt-limb charcoal, his paper blacked with the scratching *Kaa* of crows, scream of the darkness at the back of the throat that shafts down past the heart, where everything goes when swallowed.[†]

---

[*]   *Maison de Tolerance*: Brothel
[†]   Van Gogh was a Christian missionary in the Belgian coalfields before he became an artist.

The Poet, the Lover, of Van Gogh

1. We Meet

I am Dutch, of course.

He follows me to my father's allotment,
windmills, giant crucifixions
spinning out the northerlies.
His eyes have the quality of spades dug inward.
"I am a thistle," he prays,
"about to be uprooted."

Doodle crows, schoolboy crows, twin chevrons:
thought waves gone wrong.
His entire face musters
          (a murder of crows)
The dried nape of a sun-flower makes him cry,
wheat-hard severed stump
the circumference of my wrist.

2. In Arles

Always these sun-flowers in the water.
He lifts the jug's porcelain belly, oystered breast,
And I suck clear milk from beneath the leaves;
seed-filled faces shine my skin, yellow
(laughter) brushes my temple.
His fingers push red
hair around my ears, leaving colour, umber
shadows, his hands

baptize, muse over my brows
paint it is me who is mad (to be with him)
from this skull through the green
poison vines in my forearms

and still
my daughter sits for him
among the pumpkins and lemons like the sun.

3. Possession/Madness

His infiltrated eye.

On the moon, he'd paint in shades of dust —
        (a rose takes him, a curdle of oil, a blue-bottle).
He does not go mad in London rain
but in the Midi, the hot noon, Arles and
environs, his soul pours
to burn with the waves
holding a turquoise of water in his mouth, the sea
kisses too deeply

like the streaming roads, the right-of-ways (anathema to stray)
so planted with limes, plane trees:
highways of colour

and grasses singing their notes, quiver green, blessed green, each
one sawing, an insect on his skin, animate, multiplied: how many
drops of dew (tiny lenses) per life, the conspiracy of alluding
— magenta, mustard, olive and silver, lilac calling the swallows,
the blue-black hum of night sky, the burst of crisp brown seed-
pods, the river is and is not thunder, is not drowning

and poppies well in the field
all punctures.

*4. Want After Suicide**

The night in my head is your night.

Stars are entities, somewhere between mind and peony,
always a church steepling up, and bells,
my heart a wet stone.

Dream —
> kisses, scarlet, come from your mouth
> tongue smooth, olive-dark,
> swirling cumulus behind almond blossoms
> soil the colour of your instep, clay,
> raw porcelain among the cypresses.

Sleep —
> your brow on my collarbone

Blue —
> weeps through my face beneath the skin

waterfalls
petals fall, membranes
gun-shot hollyhocks and bindweed:
other eyes
closing.

---

*   Before he went to Arles, Van Gogh lived with a prostitute named Siene
in an attempt to "save" her. This poem is from her perspective.

One more thing to do on your birthday

Visit the morgue, not simply
to gaze. The bodies

stored like sheet music
after you refuse to play

the piano and someone stops
paying for lessons (each note is

eventually the same, one long
drawer closing);

not simply to contemplate
years buckled on steel bedding,

or to think so many *should haves*;
not simply to see

your mother's mother
balanced like a sunset, horizoned

heart of a pioneer who asks
while breaking ground: how

do we lead a good life? Each of us
repeats the question, an inquest

deepening into days detached
from everything and infinitely

folding us in the middle.

Fast Forward

A phone call from an imaginary friend

Hello: he says. *I miss you.*
And a minute or two
quiets me at first

my hand to the phone, my mouth
formation and function, surprise
ringing as my own admission:

I'm sorry, you must have
the wrong number. This isn't
911. Your emergency is nothing
but a fistful of distance.

But then he always knew
which button started the engine

his voice a leg on each side
of the landscape, sentences chauffeured along

girdled channels and fettered
possibility, his remark an opening
politeness pressed in my ear.

Hello: he says again.
I thought I'd lost you.

And the pause in the road is real
the highway empty, silence
potholed and heavy.

I respond as if I could
balance this vehicle, hesitation
a butt crease in the red
crushed lining of the seat
every velvet thread my future
listening to my past

my hair parted in the middle
and the flip back to a style
long forgotten —
some nervous dance, or one
youthful craze memorized
like a phone number
dialled late one night
in earnest.

A Letter to Jorie Graham

An answer isn't expectation,
isn't knitted from the yarn

of any poet's words. Isn't everything
something? There's usually a *why*

and an *oh*, each of these sometimes
spidery, sometimes eight different paths

that channel my brain, gesture with parted legs.
Each one a foot or two plotted institutionally

like a house on the low prairie field,
an erection of wood and glass, something

birds stare at, flap into, circle
like an interruption of interest.

(I'm building something like it.)
Not imitation, or repetition,

just easy movement,
a hawk, crow, or even the robin

at five, then four, then three
every morning. The word's turn

synchronized, seasoning
its way through months until

even the days begin to hide
somewhere underneath, laugh

at the green north side, frozen
features wasting away. A facade

realizes its own alter ego, leans
a mole nose against the backside

like an address, one place
to the other, my forehead

to paper, horizontal sense of blue stretched
skin and veins and ink.

Two Shores

The blue-green river shimmers in the heat
just as it did five years ago when I stood
on this same shore. I could almost believe
that you're waiting somewhere for me —
at the kitchen table slicing beets
or on the front steps shelling peas.

Above the river a crow calls and is gone.
I close my eyes: somewhere I am coming toward you
with a bag of oranges; you drop peas into a bowl.
Soon, I will sit beside you with the oranges at your feet
and look out at the evening sky as if there were
nothing unordinary about this.

Premonitions

In late summer, elm leaves tapping on the window
make the same sound as the rain about to fall.
Somewhere you are coming toward me, although
I don't yet know this. I don't have any premonitions
of Spanish poetry and coffee, of banana plantations
that shimmer in heat waves at the height of summer.
All I know right now is the low rumble of thunder
outside my bedroom window and the electric air
gathering before the storm.

Things that Happen in the Middle of the Night

Once she stood in a yard of tall grass. The wind chased a wisp of hair across her cheek. Behind her, a white shirt flapped on a clothesline. She was five years old and she wore her father's spectacles. Her younger brother held her hand and pretended to smoke their father's pipe. A camera caught the small black dog beside her in mid-jump.

One morning 73 years later she wakes and remembers how in the middle of the night she let that Scamp scramble up onto her bed and from then on how that dog followed her everywhere. But she forgets about the younger brother. Does not recognize him in the photograph. Wonders who he is. Likely a neighbour boy.

Highway #8 for my Dad

I would have taken a photo of the sign along the highway: *Visit the Hank Snow Centre of Country Music in Downtown Liverpool.* I think you liked Hank Snow. I think one summer we drove up to the exhibition just to hear Hank sing at the evening Grand Stand. Maybe you listened to Hank on your tractor radio. I would have developed the photo using a rebate neg holder to give it a classy *film noir* look to contrast with the kitschy-ness of a Hank Snow Country Music Centre. I would hang the photo in the upstairs hall and when people would ask about it I could say *this is a photo that reminds me of my dad.* And beside it I would hang the black and white photo of you standing with your sister Maudie in the tall grass, pretending to smoke your father's pipe.

The Boatman of Pichavaram

There is a murder in the silence here.
A groan withheld, a weight.
A thousand suns bear down on his skin — looking at him
you know — this lead sunlight
has molded every pore
so he moves like leaves
but needs to rest after an hour of rowing.
His legs are small as a child's —
his calves half the size of mine.
The top of his head
just reaches my shoulder.
I wonder how often he has been hungry,
and who can carry the heavier weight.

This man carries a heat inside him,
something melted, then soldered
altered in how one molecule joins another —
now hard and bright in his centre — cold brass
glowing as a polished sun, ready to explode —

Rajasthani

Butter-tongue stones roil upwards in white-hot sunlight. Women dress in desert sands' refracted rays, Earth's scattered voices, pink, yellow, orange, laugh in their veils. Bone-white columns of bracelets rattle in leaf-bare shadow-webs of wind-skinned branches. Drought-twisted trees' bleached minds have given up despair. In a mud-walled circle with a thatch roof a woman washes rice, washes rice, strains the water in a pot — uses it to wash her own face and arms. The sand whirls outside and a brown and white bird in the rafters says hello. Cowrie shells from distant oceans ornament her sleeves. Home comes from watching the sun rise every day, feeding goats, carrying water in a clay pot, needing flowers. Her ancestors' palace is jungles of carved petals and leaves. By stone's grace I smell lilies and jasmine in sandstone acrid dust, in the hot wind-smell of dung. Symmetry and longing entwine in columns, in gold-flowered arches and mosaic domes. You, desert woman, you shape your dreams in shelves of mud and paper, painted white. Broken bangles glint colour. Bits of mirror glimpse who you might have been, in a brief section of jaw, in the shadow under your lip. You kiss your son's forehead and laugh at a brother's joke. The grief in your eyes is never spoken, never hid. Tell me your faraway places.

A Woman Sleeps with Winter

A woman sleeps with winter,
frosty toes and fingers stinging
her back in the warmth
of a shared bed.
She curses the pitiful shivering
of one so strong,
little to be done but
live with the inclement
bastard until his mood
changes yet again.

But I greet winter
as respite from doing —
planting, worrying,
harvesting,
hoping.

Winter is a constant
fury, predictable
like the goose down comforter
wrapped round our frigid
selves released
from the numbing effects
of endless work,
the great equalizing
blanket of snow white
snow enveloping us
until finally we are
warm.

Pockets and Sparrows

Especially in January, swollen footprints,
scraps of frost, are signatures
in the forest guestbook. Initials on paper
scented with sparrows.

This is where I sign in, spill pockets
of blackened bullets. My skittish hand
shakes past the tree line.

Lungs are purest here.
But in the city, plastic
grips the branches like birds.

Slow Woman

saundered down my childhood
streets, carried her secret age
and patient diseases. Time entered her
through every unhurried avenue, leaving
flaps of walrus-like wrinkles.
I imagined ashen hairs breaking
each night she unraveled
her tight bun.
                    Hush, hush, hush.
My eight-year-old back, resting
against an elm's torso, I was pushed
into the soft dough of sleep
with each of her steps.
                    Hush, hush, hush.

I followed her to the Jehovah's Witness
Hall, her Fourth Ave apartment,
sun breaking on black
birth-marked cheeks, a grin full of gums, teeth
hanging out in the heat. Her gigantic butt
in floral housedresses.
That swaying.

January

When your train arrived from Luton,
I was wandering among the bodies
rolling into shops, out of trains, King's Cross
a human river, all obstruction. Still,

you found me in the station
in front of Sainsbury's, orange sign
tinting my black coat. Your greeting:
one kiss, on each cheek.

Last August I woke at six,
the morning new as our coupling,
and I caterpillared from under your arm,
drank mimosas on your balcony
the fizz like static on the tongue.

Later, we caught a taxi
across Petofi bridge. Your Irish brogue
sung broken Hungarian,
a ballad clipped into staccato;
sibilance, lost fish
pushing upstream in the Danube.

Now, on the news the north is flooding.
I curl into hotel sheets, sick with a trickle
of a chill. Rain bangs against our window,
even this far south, but you pull the drapes
and we cocoon here, out of the current.

Elizabeth's Monologue: The Metal Mannequin[*]

It holds court in my boudoir.
Dress the iron body with jewelry;
my sapphire bracelet, that old
pewter crown.
                        The way you
skitter back makes me wonder
if you heard last night's girl.
Your fear draws me like French perfume,

wafts from your fine skin, sixteen years
of uselessness. Your beauty
has no titles, no muscle, no consequence
except to lure a merchant's son,
or stoke my stable boys. Your pale hair
is a false promise of gold, your Slovak
voice a cheap load of tin.

Now, take the necklace. Circle your arms,
fasten this string of diamonds at the nape.
At last, the click — my lady attacks.

Your cry excites me like a lover's caress
as the steel spike penetrates
your suckle-soft abdomen. I cup
your wound, reap
the red treasure I've released.

You writhe like a deliciously wounded deer,
blood wetting your lips.
My kiss collects this spill.

---

[*]   Elizabeth Bathory, 16th century Hungarian countess, murdered her
      servant girls and reportedly bathed in their blood in hopes of keeping
      her skin youthful looking.

Still Life

in his last days
my father could eat only pears
not familiar Bartletts
but Boscs with bloodred skin
pale flesh tender in his mouth

one day the fruit lay untouched
in an earthen bowl
each pear seeded
with dark decay

maskîhkiy âstôtin

Blackfoot blackened out Cree footsteps
surrounded, cut off all paths
beside the river they moved
up against banks
like *kâ-monakos*, "Male Weasel"
had a pretty daughter
nipayi-miyosit
terribly beautiful

Blackfoot took to words
with guns loaded
river pushed down the sky
the Blackfoot leader said
"We will leave you alone
If you let me have your daughter"
"*moya*. No. You cannot have her"
the chief said
He loved her too much

he threw his bonnet in the river
and it was called
maskîhkiy âstôtin, Medicine Hat
Crees went to their camp
along the river
nêhiyawak in the camp
began to wonder what would happen

ispihk ê-wî-pê-sâkâstêk
when the dawn would come
fires raced to the skies
veterans told stories
to steady the nerves of the young ones
kâ-monakos, Male Weasel
ê-kî-nêhiyawâtamot
sang his Cree song
called his helper,
kinêpik, snake
dug into earth
created a pathway through the earth
tunnel snuck past Blackfoot lines
emptied the camp
ê-pê-sâkâstêk
when the dawn would come
left the Blackfoot no one to fight

cîhcam

cîhcam daughter of *masâskâpaw*
"toes touching the bottom of the water"
my uncle Burton Vandall told me
water never leaving the sight of sky

cîhcam, her body was our blanket
gave us life and language
brought stars from the sky
brought our souls from deep oceans
to the water of our birth
cîhcam was *mosôm*'s Gabriel's mother
cîhcam was grandmother to us all

there is a book written
blue binding and loose stitching
about her uncle *atâhk-akohp*
the northern Starblanket
from around Prince Albert
black drawings
with boxes of connects
name her as "unknown daughter"
but we know her as *kôhkom cîhcam*

cîhcam did not take Treaty
êkâ ê-âkimiht, "not counted"
not counted by Treaty
as my father and Uncle Burton used to say
some of our relatives lived by *waskisiw*
their hunting ground
place of rest in the world
lived in bush
trademarked now as a park

Grey Owl chased out Indians
to save the Beaver
movie-reel Indians
chase Real Indians
from folds of lakes
and curves of bush

land becomes heavy
with new words
old stories become distant
quiet whispers in tired mouths
new names fill the trees
games laws cut trap lines
iron tracks pass over
lines of hunter's sleep

wind across the body
dries my cracking limbs
heavy like trees
can no longer trace the stars
in the sky
nor bring the water to the sky
old names become cold whispers
from our cold mouths
which can no longer speak
old name memories

cîhcam, her words and stories
raise the earth through her lips
under her kitchen table
thrown blanket over
put rocks on skillet floor
improvised ceremony

Fast Forward

cîhcam gave back air to lungs
sun back to sky
brings us home
sanctuary of stories
and thick Cree poems
she is our blanket
of stars and takes us
to the edge of words
and the beginning of songs

stories, like small animals
gather pieces of green trees
make limbs alive again
bring water from distant waters
moisten my failing dry flesh
becomes river again
gives warmth to our lips
and old names

she kept songs
ancient poetic pathways
take us to stars
to the top of stars
to the bottom of water

she lived until the 1950s
died at the age
of 110 or so
we are her living body
storytellers and poets
hold traces of her
her stories and words
warm us
with blankets of stars
wake sleeping water
to the sky

Pow Wow Wives

My girl is pow wow crazy
crazy shaking jingles
French braids tied back
tâpwê tight
call it her Indian botox surgery

we head out to pow wows
chairs duct taped on the roof
½ tank of gas
bologna sandwiches
we fly through country
dust flying, rez dogs
barking, chasing our path

she can do it all
braiding her hair
smoking, beading
last minute additions
playing radio bingo
at the same time
stakats boy!
how does this creelicious
delicious, mischievous
neechi woman
do it? wow

I have one tip though
as a neechi man
walking around the Pow Wow arbours
rounding the rounds
remember . . .
Indian women
respect hickies
more than wedding rings

Pelvis

The pelvis speaks a small sentence
hips sigh a spread of hesitation
center of gravity shifts
small fetus sleeps
within a womb waiting

The pelvis groans
more room please
the hips and greater trochanter stretch the skin of the drum
belly ballooning of seven months

The pelvis speaks a small sentence
piriformis is pushing pressure
on sciatic nerve

The pelvis moans today
my hands restore the ligaments and tendons
allowing for rest before the pelvis shouts
it is time it is time

Island

Emma shifts from paper to the canvas
priming it like an old lover
her movement soothing   almost thoughtless
She uses words like *medium*   *subject matter*
when she means paint   the lake   the sky

She controls the canvas
blank   unformed until her hands
mark him   a slash   a brand
a smudge

I am telling Emma
I used to have a lover
who held his lips like you
I don't care how she takes this
strike a match   shake it out
My lover, well, my husband really
was a painter too
She has stopped listening
mesmerized by the island horizon
a gray on black she'll try again in the morning
when it is light enough for shadows

I am wrestling ghosts in this darkness
each one still real enough for me to dream his name
I will murmur their names while awaking
They visit in the dreams lost last night
That's how I run from them
How I invoke them
always the distant islands
A woman who sees lovers
in the lips of a stranger
lives in shadows long gone cold

Emma drifts to her cabin bed
my feet stretch though moon-gray sand
my body numb   my hands cupped
over the red end of a cigarette
For a moment   through the smoke
in the cave of my fingers
the plains of my palm are blank

Billie Holiday: the chair

My grandmother sits in a chair.
If she lies down she will die.
I look out the window.
She asks me to spread a blanket
on the floor and lie with her.
I love her so much, but I tell her no.
She insists and I can't stand her crying.

I lay the grey blanket on the wooden floor,
lift her from the chair, stretch her out on the floor
and she talks to me and laughs and I sleep.

Five hours later I wake up, my neck stiff,
wrapped tight with grandma's arm.
I can't move and grandma's eyes
stare white facing the window.

The neighbours had to break her arm
to let me loose.
They left grandma in the front room
for the wake.
They took me to the hospital.
When I returned my cousin beat me
for letting grandma out of the chair.

The chair sits in the corner
by the window.
Sometimes I sleep in it
humming fragments of song.

Billie Holiday: the red dress

On account of a man
I was sentenced to the Catholic institution
where the nuns never ventured beyond the wall.

I wore the ragged red dress the first time
as punishment at Easter.
The other girls weren't allowed near me.
My mother brought a basket of chicken
and the nuns made me watch the other girls eat it.

At night I wasn't allowed to sleep with the others.
The sisters locked me in the room with the dead girl,
who broke her neck, trying to fly from the swing,
wearing the same red dress I now wore.

In the dark I pounded at the door.
All night my screams echoed the halls.
Blood filled my fingernails.
I thought I could hear the dead girl whisper.

I still hate closed doors.
When I sing, the doors are wide open,
and people come in and out, laughing.

The Cellophane Sky

Duke at the window
lights low above the Paris streets
sipping a sugared Coca-Cola
sitting in the night, his night.
His pants undone, belly loose,
now finally alone
after visitors and room service,
steak frite and a half bottle of red,
the Countess already asleep.

A woman's high heels echo on cobble
Duke taps out the rhythm on the window ledge,
moves to the portable electric piano
working out the tone of foot steps
with the high notes.

His eyes follow the street lights,
a string of pearls, to a dark horizon line.
He waits for the cellophane sky,
the first few seconds of pale light
as dawn breaks and night and day merge.
"Looking for heaven, always have been."
Now he can sleep.

My Father's Aunt Was Hanging Wash on the Line
Her Children Were Playing in the Yard

Aunt Helen, on the day the young soldier
held that cold metal gun to your head
and demanded a cup of tea or he would kill you
the world stood still for your children

The baby stopped crying
your oldest daughter whispered prayers
all your children froze in horror
everyone held their breath

When you looked into his blue eyes
and said, "No," I imagine the birds stopped
in midflight, every blade of grass stayed still
the weather vane stopped squeaking

Even the bees stopped buzzing
All was silent while his eyes fought
a battle of wills with you and he lost
lowered the gun and walked down the street

and out of town. The way gunslingers
do in the movies, his feet scuffing up
dust as he left. The sun beating down
on his head wind ruffling his hair

You watched as he became smaller then was gone
Aunt Helen not many would have been so brave
You made the birds fly again, the wind blow
and the bees come back out from the hive

Money Orders

I have memorized every word
on these pieces of paper
receipts issued to my grandfather
money sent to his girlfriend
planning to join him in Canada

This woman is legend
in my family issuing a curse
upon him, his wife, his
children when she learned
of his new relationship

Curses cannot cross water
they say, her fury was
greater than any body of water
this woman no longer
wanted or needed in the new world

It worked. Early deaths
became the fate
of my grandparents, suffering
pain and illness in a land
that promised luxury and
long life. Their first born dead at birth
Their second tumbled the length
of the basement stairs
his head a watermelon
hitting concrete
The daughter suffers the loneliness
of outliving all of her family

She must not have cursed
the rest of us, or there was
a time expiry, perhaps
she died. I like to think
she found happiness and
released us all

Artifacts

I'm digging through records
sifting through time for relevant
facts and information
Archæology of the family

Painstakingly, carefully
I send for birth certificates
death certificates, marriage registrations
immigration records, church metrical books

Polish, German, Latin, Ukrainian, English
I am a smattering-lingual, know
vital terms in five languages:
born, died, mother, widow, son, daughter
midwife, legitimate, not legitimate
the little crosses beside the birth
registration need no words, no language

I acquire my grandfather's army papers
my grandmother's bible
pictures of people important to me
whom I've never met
A cassette tape that stored
my grandmother's voice
thirty years ago and by chance
somehow caught a family fight

It is always this kind of treasure
the searcher looks for
the personalities
behind vital events
the tombstone information
This artifact, the priceless gem
in my collection

Fast Forward

We Light Red Candles

                  turn the air cinnamon,
sandalwood — autumn shadows climb
these walls, thin shivers of smoke
waver like starlight,
laughing flames whisper:

      winter is riding the wind

You carry a cluster of apples
cupped in a bowl, old wood —
memory colours its rings like veins.

My summer hands slip
on the smooth skin of Delicious;
silver-toothed blade flashes
through flesh, crisp and white,
removes the stump of the core.

I crave soft sandings of sugar,
plump gold raisins scattered like coins,
leaf-crackle of walnut, pecan,
trickle of honey, spilled sap in dusky woods.

         winter is riding the wind

It is now I must remember
how smell is swallowed by the body,
the way *brown* melts like butter,
your mouth, a blessing of scent.

A Poet Prepares

I've been thinking keep it simple, stupid
Yeah, just make 'em laugh if I can
Tell 'em how I come from the prairies
A land so flat that when your wife walks out
You can watch her leave for three whole days
I'm thinking make 'em laugh 'cause
Comedy pays better than tragedy and
It surely as hell costs less

So yeah make 'em laugh
Though I'm flirting too with a political theme
Something in a post-modern style with a
Bruce Cockburn reference about
Lovers in a dangerous time
Layer in Bogie and Bergman, the airstrip in Casablanca
The troubles of three little people, their little hill of beans
(A po-mo pastiche, why not?
'Cause every line I steal is one I don't have to write)
Salt in some not-so-surreal image of lovers on a melting ice-cap
(they are, remember, melting)
build the climax around a final cell call on September 11th
goodbye my sweet goodbye
A dicey move I know
They might bitch and hiss how I mock the dead when
I mean to mock the living
Politics as usual
Business as usual
The body-count mounts
Goodbye my friends goodbye

Or I could simply go 100 proof confessional
Autobiographical
Pure-grain alcohol honesty —
But I don't want to go up on charges
Again.

I also have this Norman Mailer bit I haven't used in awhile
Juggle some knives for the edification of the crowd
(he stabbed his wife, you know, his second wife, or was it his third?)
But spin it around, say yeah, my Ex she cleaned me out
Took the toothpaste and the laundry soap
Took the family dog and the family jewels
Yeah she bailed out with the cutlery
Though the knife in my back
She *was* sweet enough to leave
I could go with that old trick
It's worked before
Though not with that lesbian in the audience
In Whitehorse

And since we've landed on that particular landmine
I could tell them of a lovely bi-sexual woman who
Shared my Nova Scotia bed
How together we grew corn and baled hay
Fed the goats
milked the cows
Fixed the barn roof
How I pushed her over the edge
Accidentally of course
No, not over the edge of the roof
Over the edge sexually
After me she's no longer bi
After me she only sleeps with women
(It's always good to tell a story against yourself
Gets the crowd on-side)

Well
Except for that reading in Whitehorse

I've been working too on a cowboy show
A splash of Hank
a shot of Wilco
A snort of Emmylou
Something along the lines of
"I was three days out of detox
When I seen her face again
She was standing on the corner of River Street
With the man who'd been my friend"
I'm thinking of maybe doing blue-collar cowboy
How the phone don't ring
And the door don't knock
Pedal steel blues
Three chords and the truth
If only to irritate the hip-hop crowd

If I get truly blocked
I could dig out some lyric fragments from the drawer
Like Tom Waits who calls 'em car parts in the back yard
"Hey, this carb from the Dodge'll work in the Chevy"
Well I got car parts
Here's one:
"She took a cynic to her bed
She stroked his sneer till I purred in the dawn
And though she was not the first
I swear by the God I had as a child
It was never making love until then"
And if I tell 'em I wrote those words
On a lunch bag
On the night shift
In a lead smelter
A blast furnace inferno with
The foreman bellowing in Portuguese

Well, maybe it'll seem like a better thing
Than a brake shoe rusting in the yard

Or maybe
Maybe I'll just say this:
That before the movie starts
When the lights are going down
You clap your hands, hoping
You clap your hands because
the movie just might be good this time
because a happy ending is still possible

Maybe I'll just say
That when you don't think I'm watching
You sing to the food on the table
That high off the hog or scraping on the dole
You bless our soup with a homemade song
And hold me in a state of grace

Yeah
Maybe I'll just say that
Keep it simple

Driving down into Qu'Appelle

late October, following
the slow curve of this road

there is a place, where the hills
meet — lie together
where the trees form a dark triangle
opening up to the horizon

I know a part of you, he says
that looks like that

I run my fingers
over the rough grain of his jeans
imagine small birds in that place
fluttering over naked branches

Nocturne

over the shallow sound
of your breath on my neck
I can hear the moths
humming
in your window
humming between
the blind
and the glass

they keep me awake
I don't want to wake you

in the morning
as you have your cigarette
I'll gather their bodies
my cupped hands full
soft torsos silk wings
dark again
and still

Ghazal: waxwing

tsee-tsee, to see, to sleep, to dream, to smoke the night's
last cigarette, to see, to quote the waxwing

this winter, you can see the stars again, the orange light of the city
rises in the east, and falls on the coat of the waxwing

the December wind scattered tiny apples, fermented blood on snow,
frozen, then warmed in the throat of the waxwing

we breathe the prairie silence, the cold dark sky, listen
to the wind beneath songs of the coyote and the waxwing

the branches of the tree hold their bodies, flutter, give
darkness the last trill note of the waxwing

when you slip into bed, kiss the curve of my neck,
Poet, I say, *who wrote of the waxwing?*

Trembling Aspen

Through each leaf, swollen sun, thin-mapping
vein, the first angles of a girl
stirring. This is all I need to stay, an idea
of water serving light, eyelids in their first pull
of sky, a single line in crayon, erratic blue
circles. Your first veins
running down each breast, claw marks
in dirt, pathways I don't want to see, the heart
held to the light, the chained
rays of blood.

    ∞

You head out to the aspen trail and down,
down to the dried flower moss, the imprints
of a child, hoof or paw. You don't read tracks,
just the depressions, a slope of weight
on its turn, the deepening lines of doubt.

    ∞

Gold wind aspen waltz, back-of-arm listening. This is the heart
in a treetop swaying to a noon sun that drips to the ends of a root
and pulses off a leaf that skipping-song-skips all the way to your door.

This is that which never ends, water
small-kissing stone, skin stretched to your amazement
without bursting, the heart
weak from her first complete circle, the pivot of her entire body,
shoulders and hips, and a line, so simple, coming around.

This is the thin, backlit song, song of the globed
blonde-feathered seed, song of unrooted
memory, a stain of wing
at the back of the eye, the bird you couldn't save
and the worm tunneling its throat, the worm inside
hunger dying, over and over in the restless earth, the toil
of small, still organs.

∞

Anything that dusts, moulds, soaks up the earth and grows a new
sky. Anything that dies by breaking off from a fine point and
flying for the first time with a one-of-a-kind map of a tree
embedded in its back. Anything with luck, a last shadow that rou-
lette-twirls its body from palm to heartline to dust.

∞

I want hair the colour of the flametip on the stem
of a leaf that has blackened, the sweet edge
she brought to me, folded in her pocket, the pressed
air-damp of deer trail moss. I want

a map of roots when you hold me to the light, freckled
sun, that pile dad buries us in, little red maple hearts
throbbing sky. I want the hush
of the rake, the impossibility of gathering,
the one that lands and splits
at the spine, the matching halves.

I want two quilts stitched into yellow
hearts then torn, a seam
with the patience of a line, a book
written on one single leaf. To be
the one she finds when she turns
to make her way home.

∞

A bead of water, your face
in the dew-tip of a leaf, grass
broken in hoof and weight, in the first weave
of nest. What it means to return
to a place you have never been, an angle of sky
you are seeing for the first time, leaves,
leaves after rain, all that gold dizziness.

See me here, only halfway descended, turning
back up the clay slick, jumping at every stump
hunched, bear scat studded in rosehips
and crows overhead winging their black snouts,
huffing, deep-chested I am telling myself *don't run.*

Running now, running because the last time
I played dead there was blood and regret there was
animal breath up the neck and an ear pressed to the phone.
There was wire, snail-coiled and the inching up
of red-digit eyes, a corner of starless
night in your back pocket, tucked
like a photo you don't want to share
or a wish you've over-memorized so that the meaning has fallen, so
that the words are the wish, so that the saying of it is the wish, so
that the eyes closed
are syllable, deafness, one way of breathing.

∞

I am saying to you *now*
I am saying *turn over*
I am saying *sleep, babygirl, sleep*

∞

I want to stay until all the leaves shiver
off, until the path turns beneath hoof and the camera fisheye-traces
the long o of the moon. I want to stay
until after we are out of food and just before
we kill, when we have tried once and failed — that
kind of hunger. I want to walk alone into a night forest
toward a point of no light, until morning saves us
too many times.

∞

The last time there was rain, an eagle birch-circling
skulls, stone sucked from cold mudcheeks, little faces
on the underside, smiling. Now, two fish I don't see, jumping
toads, the inner-cheek of a bog that holds one foot
under, land that will be drilled for diamonds, brilliance
that will forget, tunneled and cored
its child graves, wide as a leg that has been buried
and dragged out.

∞

Forest sway, the tapering off
of every live thing, the thinnest points   eyelash, heat
the spider tying off its web. I am not finding
the warm grip of metal after you leave. A place you might have
    touched
could you remember. The invisible belly of each leaf
when the sky shines through, that socket
of warmth cupped to the eyes, the sudden strangeness
of a voice you've known all your life that makes you think
of eggs, soft-boiled, the spooned light of yoke
blurring on the tongue. I am not finding what drifts
like a fog across the lens, what you have folded
so carefully, arm by arm and placed to your chest, the family
disappearing from the room, a room that refuses to give back
your glasses, *where are the glasses?*, the ones you cover up and grip,

that I am afraid to point to because I don't know what it feels like
to be there, inside your hand, inside a palm that forgets
so tenderly, everything it holds.

∞

There is a bear we will never see
getting fat on ant hills and rosehips,
a darkness that passes a hand
in front of your face in the night, the breath
of your daughter a thousand miles away
dreaming. There is a fingerprint
beneath stone, your grandfather's just before the cub
took to his wife's breast and just after
the laying of small bones. There is the trace
of a clean hand somewhere, little black moons
trapped under a nail, the braille
of a worm in a fallen cross, bark
like a carcass slung over his shoulder, leaves
the colour of that which isn't ready.

∞

You walk with the weak-knee after-tremor of a near accident,
whitetails beaming their half-moon flight, or the head-on
sparrow-swoop before window, fear that thin, that silent.

You walk with a weather that greets you like cold arms
around your neck, a wind louder than your heart, leaves
on your shoulders like two hands holding on piggyback.

You walk away from aspen, its bark twisted like a stocking
over an old woman's ankle, from a sky opening like a broken cattle
    fence that says *runrun*,
from the dog you let off leash and his constant pull to turn you home.

∞

Dew, just before frost, a glass sun.
At the fringe of a deer bed, grass
half-bent, or our bed in the early hours
damp-lit, stroking your forehead, forgiving
a question you will never know you had.

Bald light of the clearing, back-of-leaves ghost
in the two-foot radius of ground you keep
when you walk into the light. Leaves
pressed into sand, red ribbons someone has dropped,
ruby heels clicking.

∞

If I write you a story will you take it with you and enter
unafraid, place each page behind you like a footprint, would you
    remember
to turn and read your way home, would you remember home?

If we are walking, feeling everything behind, leaf shadow
down our backs, poplar pulling all its golden ribbons,
tell me there are things you will never forget: your daughter's
    hands slipped
into mittens, the sparrowfeather of her hair after water, the lake
    circling
your ankles, a freckle on your knee as you run down the gravel
    lane, shining.

∞

There is a place on your breast that will never age, the back of a leaf
freshly dying, placed to the heart, a silk areola rounding out
the learning of small mouths.

There is a day leaf-dimming behind you, light shriveling forward,
an aspen at the bottom of the mountain and I'm wondering if it is
still burning.

There is a stairway at the top
of breath, a keyhole the stone face of a doe,
a cemetery with gold ponds and fish
wingless, flying.

There is a pulse
between trees, a grave of pillow-cornered
stone, a mother's arm
of disturbed earth cradling
blooms of lichen, nipple-crusted sap.

∞

The almost-blue
of what is not there:
cross-section of river, clear water
lens of the cow's eye you palmed
in Grade 8 biology like crystal.

Sky, a leaf dying
inside a doe's spooned listening, its tilted
eye making me want to save
what I haven't yet found.

On the green side of the mountain
a little gold door

you wait to enter.

Birds, Pity Nostradamus

Domine, forgive me my memories — a strange
thought to enter the snail of the head.

An old man makes soup much like a child would, if only
to tolerate the afternoons. And cleans himself with candles.

Months or years, feel the fish-cold stone. The first of night's
flagships is a kitchen's worn down floor.

Birds, pity Nostradamus, locked into the future, and
forced to take all of its fierceness down.

Prophecy isn't tennis, isn't a star's vacant steps, isn't
a table one face deep. Is a collection of missing fingerprints.

But the past is, the past is, the past is an enclosure,
a change room only a few of us have ever seen.

And new love/she's wearing smiling skulls on her finest boxers,
never, never to cradle suicide's astonished microphone.

A Woman was Given a Choice

You can be someone who can hear
the sea's face shadowed with rain, the delayed
generosity of clouds and other blind
things/or you can have a voice

that turns a graveyard into a piano
being played across a lake. It's that
brutal, every season's
renunciation.

The Colour White

begins with eggshell.
Surrender's wave. Knotted

underwear, worn on
the cross. The baby teeth
your father kept for you
in a Japanese box.

Thanks for visiting. Come again.

2.

The colour white is popcorn
on the floor — seeds forgotten
from childhood, if childhood could
ever have been a movie. Because

the colour white makes illness
easier, check out the fingernails
of everyone here. Because the colour white, when
careless, churns out aphorisms, check
out that Russian painter, the one
whose brush tore the drama
from monologue — its
blood blown across
the scarcest snow.

What's the hurry?

3.

I lie in a red box. A torso
for collectors only. Wax over
Bisque porcelain. My hair, they
say, could be human.

What's your hurry?

Every love song is
flour between your fingers.

4.

Bleached. The sun's a violin.
An owl's claw. And the soul
suspends its worth. The colour white
looks up at you from face down on a deluged
sidewalk. Reflected, trees initiate. Shepherd infinitude
into dimensions of rising cloud. White, always
beyond the whispered return of
stolen things / Staring, the colour
white reels inside
us:

5.

an elderly Jewish woman on TV last night gave me this gift, a
mitzvah that I'm passing on to you. After surviving the camps, she
found herself destitute in what remained of Europe. She fell in love
with a man. He fell in love with her. They wanted to get married,
and she felt bad that she couldn't have a wedding like the ones
she remembered from her childhood. Her husband-to-be promised
her a white wedding dress. But how to get one? His response: with
a kilo of coffee and some cigarettes he bought a parachute on the
black market. It had once been used by the Nazis. He dragged the
parachute, a silk cloud, across recurrent fields to a tailor, who then
fashioned a virginal dress from the material. She was married in it.
And so, eventually, were seventeen other brides.

Excerpts from *Mesner's Dead:*
Photo of a Reflection on Coming Clean

iv. [photo of the reflection of an ear]

Mesner sits at his kitchen table
with a cup of coffee and one
of the booklets he was given
for guidance. He reads aloud phrases
into a light the evening
will later burn black
but in that morning is a slight moss
reclining in grey.
              "Support from the partner
is the partner's sole point," he reads,
"the silent support of an ear." "If you
feel tempted to drink:
Call!" The passages rise on his voice
but (stifled by the intransigence
of cupboards and tile) call forth
no other voice but his own voice bearing
the charm of hung bells frustrated
by a funeral below; the warmth
of hull-numbed bells, bombed
straightway to the ocean
floor. The previous evening
he had sat at that same table
and listened to the leavings
of his support partner's voice accumulate
on the answering machine. His phone
had rung through steadily each time
to his partner's voiced unsteadiness
reaching as coins reach for a well
to wish in; but the receiver had lifted
not even once to return words to words'
solicitor, and with each ensuing call
Mesner had depended less and less

Fast Forward

on the ordering of eye or mind,
on the impetus of solidarity

or pursuit, until his listening
was a hunkered inhabitant of uninhabited
height, something pure, a particular
and perfect gesture heeding firmly
its own heeding like the only elegy
for where the elegy went awry.

vii. [photo of the reflection of a stamp]

A letter Mesner once received
from his support partner swore
that the thorny sprites we believe
with spirits we can sentence to death-
by-numbing will return vengeful
and no longer numb. The glimmer
we hope to hold in with wine will
slip free and leave us behind
in the most imprisoning
gloam. Dahlia withdrew

from her purse a pile of letters
she had failed that evening to share
with the group, and related
to Mesner how her sister
had spoken to her in no other
way. Though she handed over no
sentences for Mesner to skim
straight through, she did reveal her
sister's deliberate misspelling
of curse words: "Fcuk taht," she wrote
"drity btasrads," "Siht!" Mesner
meant to fold messages into envelopes
for Dahlia to receive but he never
once held the power to relinquish
the worship to which unwritten

words confined the labour
that left them unpenned.

xi. [photo of the reflection of a signature]

What Mesner never told
Dahlia's support group
was that when he was fourteen
his mother found the booze
and dirty magazines he'd stolen
from his stepfather. He never

told the group about
the making present she did
and splintering of his perfect,
secret whole: scolding him neither
for stealing nor for self's
favours to self, but for all
the selves she saw exploited

for one's viewing-produced
relief. He never confessed
to his fellow confessors
that in response he wrote
a letter to the editor arguing
for the pedagogical benefits
of pornography for minors

and signed his dead dad's name;
that the letter was published
to weeks of public debate
and his mother quit following
work's prescribed and paying
hours — no longer taking calls
from relatives enquiring:

"who's to blame?" Fallen
against the dryer was how
he had found her in a pile
of wet towels, shouldering
out a sound like steel clouds
scraping dehydrated sky.
Mesner did not share
with those recovering

around him the secret
that one ample push through
that basement wall
would have uncovered rotten
movements of earth, minute
larval pockets, a sluggish tune
in time tuned with the infinite pain's
asphyxiation of each finite hope.

xvii. [photo of the reflection of light]

The stage is empty of dancers, no
deep beats sirening their supple
rush, but Mesner remains on his chair
by the stage's edge, face releasing
an elated scream.
                          What Mesner believes
is God's eye downward burning
is the light knocked out earlier by a stray
coin. What Mesner believes God aims

through the evening's blurred-indigo height
is neither judgement nor love, but the pained,
pureful fact that a sanitized confession
could not even partially free the distorted

from its course — could never
fully answer each prayer for a flood
in which the drowning are freed
from all the waded-through silt
and siht.

Deaf Geography

I am Saskatchewan born,
lovely, dark, twinned with Russia.
My flesh remains on the steppes
in the young colony settling down
for the first winter with a deaf eye
to the cattle, potatoes in the cellar,
children in overalls, boiled home noodles
steaming the windows.

Lovely, I am deaf born,
a fox twinned with the hearing,
a shadow colony settling noiselessly
among these stubborn Russian Germans,
thrift and hard work.

Long ago in Russia,
wolves, dark shadows in the sparse birch
haunted the rich bourgeoisie
frozen inside the turrets of onion roofs.
Lovely, I dart out from the ice crusted homes
out onto the prairies toward the wolves
in dark consent.

Sylva

This body is strange.
The fields are not joyous
nor mysterious as I run through
the pungent stalks on white legs
my arms flailing over ears of corn.

That night, my master finds me under the bushes,
my red hair shakes over my shoulders.
I avoid his stale wet wool
while he holds the lantern over my face,
exclaims over the rancid breath of the hounds.

Is he my master because he offers me a raw steak?
The blood is high in my nostrils as he tells me
I am a vixen in a woman's body.

After days of following him with obsequious cant,
I wonder as I collapse into a cacophony of vowels
before him, should I give in,

wear this white shift, use a fork,
sleep in his fresh sheeted bed
curled between his head and knees.
Shall I never again gather the bones of a chicken
that I devoured in my own bed?

I sleep.
My master wakes me and I must eat.
Too tired with all this thinking,
this studying of my master, his ways,
his house, his people, his country.
In his synthetic air, I sleep.

My master's eyes are bored.
Vixen, you are deaf,
you are as you always were.

The Lure

In my den, I paw my thoughts
before language as if they were fond old tricks.
They are chickens easily devoured,
eggs quickly sucked into my mouth,
farmers outsmarted and hounds
thrown off my scent.

My eyes test the sun
high over my den. I see you eating
a pear, your body swaying
as you tramp through the wheat,
a young, stalwart farmer.
You must have slept in your fields that night
for a tattered blanket flaps around your legs.

You raise your arms to the sun,
and in a fit of merriment,
you adroitly flip onto your back.

Blinking, I emerge.
You are not my husband,
who is still sulking by the black pool,
feeding our hounds,
tinkering with the seeder.

You were in the orchard
hiding behind the blue black bushes.
I saw you at times, your back disappeared
into the trees, your face a mask against the sun,
a witness to the love between my husband and I,
a divine love, the one that carried me
through the lives of the saints. All that love
is a young farmer whose language
begins with our bodies imprinted on my mind.

The Pear Orchard

Mother, now that you've let me be deaf,
scraped your womb of its dank winter trees,
cleared the unkempt patches,
you've let me be a pure seed begun
in you, a room of buried longings.

Your passion sang long and hard for me,
this lushness beginning in the spring orchard.

My longings begin their fleshly protrusions,
my most wild need is heard
and is not yours, but mine

as the dream of pears accompanies me
through your seasons until the burst

of my deaf body, a blossom
through your floor, my limbs, strong green vines
push through your windows, straining
with the flesh of my stray desire:

Let me deaf, hold my ear to your breast,
let me see how the pear orchard grows.

Song

My hair once oiled your feet.
You, not I, knew what it meant.

Now you gather me, small and white,
freshly wakened from my sleep.

Please stay.
You are a tent over me,
a canopy of swallows,
and I will quickly embroider
in gold thread,
their resting and mating.

The swallows are startled into flight.
You gather me.
Now we cover the sky.

AFTERWORDS

"Stare, stare, stare":

Learning How to Read Wolverine Creek

Pussy willow
salix amygdaloides
young leaves with long silky hair

∞

Late Autumn and the light has shifted from the surfeit tones of harvest to November's sidelong glance and rumours of snow. Through the third floor classroom windows you can see the archway of elms along the road that leads to the St. Peter's Abbey graveyard and beyond that, the empty stubble fields look like the shaggy pelt of an animal beginning to grow out its winter coat. The sun has set behind a thin overcast sky and there's the molasses and yeast smell of baking bread from the Abbey's basement kitchen. Soon the Abbey bells will sound and the monks will head to vespers. Soon Tim Lilburn's philosophy class will be over and you'll make your way to the Abbey's basement dining room for a bowl of hot soup.

"I'll give fifty bucks, right now, to anyone who can name, properly name, five plants in the bluff behind the Abbey," Lilburn says. Silence doesn't descend; it actually pools at the base of things like dusk shadows until suddenly it's looming, until suddenly it's everywhere, until suddenly the class is held-breath quiet in an awkward, "is that Jason Hoffman's stomach growling?" kind of way. Palpable in the room is the collective introspective speculation about whether Lilburn is or is not a little off his rocker. After all, didn't he come to class last week sporting a black eye from (so he says) a hockey scuffle? Despite the averted, please-god-I-hope-he-doesn't-ask-me-

I-just-want-to-go-eat-some-soup gazes, Lilburn is revved. Suddenly he's by a window urgently pointing in the direction of the rigid calligraphy of poplars lining Wolverine creek. You think how his hand looks like a badger as it furtively traces the body of the creek onto the window's frost.

"C'mon guys! Fifty bucks. Why no takers?!"

∞

Slough grass
Beckmannia syzigachne
leaves 3 – 10mm wide

∞

Lawrence Buell writes that according to contemporary literary theory a writer's capacity to render a faithful mimesis of the natural world is considered to be relatively unimportant and her interest in doing so is often thought to be a secondary concern (p. 84). Literary depictions of nature are all too often thought, by critics, to exist for their symbolic or ideological attributes rather than as objects of contemplation for their own sake. Buell adds that "all major strains of literary theory have marginalized literature's referential dimension by privileging structure, textuality, ideology or some other conceptual matrix that defines the space discourse occupies as apart from factical 'reality'" (p. 86). Thus literary theory has turned the attempt to generate writing which articulates and foregrounds the environment into a puerile, untheoretical pursuit. The material world, at best, is setting — a devalued backdrop whose sole function is to help impart the text's larger, more important meaning. Upon reading Lilburn when he writes about "chokecherry dewlapped hills, / hills buffalo-shouldered with shag of pulsed heat, meek hills, / sandhills of rose-hip and aster" (p. 13), as good little soldiers of literary theory we're trained to ask questions such as: "I wonder what Lilburn *means* when he's talking about those hills. . . . I wonder what those hills *represent?*" Surely Lilburn's got an agenda; surely he's not so naïve to think his poems might actually, with language, attend to that dry scrub land along the South Saskatchewan river. Hasn't he heard the Poststructuralist assertions that the kinship between language and world has dissolved, that things and words are unforgivingly separate from each other, that writing is a discourse distinct from physical reality?

∞

Chokecherry
Prunus virginiana
medium to large multi-stemmed fruiting shrub

∞

"Stare, stare, stare hard. Let the thing come to you. Hear it." Lilburn has asked us to keep a journal for the environmental philosophy class he teaches at St. Peter's College and Abbey. Every day for a half hour we're supposed to go outside, still the nervous chatter in our minds, and jot down field notes from our looking. He offers no advice other than the seemingly cryptic command to stare, to *really* look at things, to approach them slowly as one would a head-shy animal.

Early mornings I drive my half ton down the back roads to St. Pete's for class. If there's time, I pull over at a low spot where, during wet springs, Wolverine Creek swells into the surrounding tufts of scrub bush. Here the chalky predawn light is cut by the odd angles of willows. The ecologist Stan Rowe writes that the growth of trees responds not only to the soils in which they're rooted, but equally to the aerial climate. The feral poses of the willows in slough grass are an oblation to the rising sun. Their gnarled branches are ecstatic dancers rooted to an utterly unfettered sky.

∞

Water parsnip
Sium suave
fruit has prominent ribs

∞

In "Nature and Poets" the late nineteenth-century naturalist and essayist Augustus Burroughs writes that "the greater the poet, the more correct and truthful will be his specifications" (quoted in Buell, p. 88). Buell writes that in his tour of poetically rendered landscapes, Burroughs reprehends writers who make ornithological and botanical blunders for the sake of the poem's internal music. Burroughs is not calling for wholesale scientific objectivity, but rather he asks writers to let the reality of their physical milieu to guide poetic intention. There are no nightingales in Kansas, no yews in Saskatchewan and Burroughs thinks it's only lesser poets whose writing is guilty of such ecological absurdities. Burrough's motto is simple: "the beautiful not *over*, but *through* the true." George Eliot affirms Burroughs sentiments when she writes that "all truth and beauty are to be attained by a humble and faithful study of nature, and not by substituting vague forms...in place of substantial reality" (quoted in Buell, p. 91).

Buell evokes these classical realist writers not to privilege their stance, but rather to point out that textual representation should be dually accountable to both matter and issues of textuality, ideology and poesis. Writing that aspires to be accountable to water parsnip and red clover refuses to allow "language" or "history" or "culture" to have its way over discourse unchecked (p. 93). Unmediated antireferentialism in the domain of literary theory mutes the very real claim that the environment has over humanity; it denies writers the project of conjuring the natural world with language and thereby it further denies readers the possibility of achieving intimacy with the world as well as the text.

∞

Red clover
Trifolium pratense
flowers are dark pink with a paler base produced
in a dense infloresence

∞

Writing that endeavours to articulate nature need not be over confident in its ability to do so; such attempts, in fact, can be predicated upon the writer's dislocation as she tries to find words for the bloodshot skins of chokecherries. Lilburn writes:

> There is a singing in things. Or you can call it a sleep. Its beauty is a kind of loyalty, an upholding, a patriotism for something that does not seem to exist. Though immense, it is frail. This shining tone in things vanishes to be replaced by sentiment and ownership as soon as any sort of relationship with it is assumed. I want this thing and this wanting will make me poor" (*Living, p. 75*).

Loyalty to the singing in things and our inevitable poverty before their ineffability does not dismiss the project of trying to write authentically about the environment; our failed attempts can be beautiful, can momentarily bridge the abyss between language and the world. "The subject of poetry," Wendell Berry writes, "is not words, it is the world, which poets have in common with other people." Despite his manifest insecurity about language's ability to fully encapsulate wilderness, when Lilburn writes about coyotes "slouch-jogging out of the moth-coloured trees down to the river / after supper" as a reader, for a moment, I feel a comradery akin to coming home (*Moosewood, p. 32*).

∞

Silverweed
Potentilla anserina
leaflets white, hairy underneath and green above

∞

I couldn't take Tim Lilburn up on his challenge that evening. Nobody could despite the fact that most of the students at St. Peter's College, myself included, grew up on nearby farms. My realization that I couldn't name five plants along the very creek that bordered my parent's land surprised me and made me feel as though I had somehow behaved rather rudely, like I was a boorish, exploitive tourist to a landscape I'd inhabited since my birth.

Why should a writer pore into the barbed heart of Canada thistle? Why make such focused looking a high priority? Deeply attending to minute facts such as the dried silverweed creeping along the banks of the Wolverine requires us "remake our world," to shift our criterion of value. Focusing on what is all too often overlooked or deemed unimportant has the effect of confirming it as just as real and important as we are (Buell, p. 107). When Lilburn writes of rose-hips "burnt red with frost," of magpies "hair-triggered and thuggish in worn trees," of wolf willow and sage, these seemingly inconsequential aspects of the environment become intensities of great worth (*Moosewood*, pp. 27, 28).

Environmental literacy grows increasingly important even as such knowledge in the public conscious grows more obscure. This, I think, was part of Lilburn's point – learn the names of things as a simple gesture of courtesy. And in the process of becoming environmentally literate, of undertaking concentrated depiction, the self is humbled and appropriative human-centric desires are stilled.

∞

Canada thistle
Cirsium arvense
an aggressive creeping perennial

WORKS CITED

Buell, Lawrence. *The Environmental Imagination: Thoreau, Nature Writing and the Formation of American Culture.* Cambridge: Harvard UP, 1995.

Lilburn, Tim. *Living in the World as if it Were Home.* Dunvegan, Ontario: Cormorant, 1999.

_____. *Moosewood Sandhills.* Toronto: McClelland & Stewart, 1994.

Rowe, Stan. *Home Place: Essays on Ecology.* Edmonton: NeWest, 1990.

POETRY AND THE BODY

The body, and issues connected to it — pain, beauty, pleasure — are common themes in literature. Poets, in particular, depend on sensual references, and visual images of the body to communicate emotion and meaning in their work. We read about, and consequently visualize, broken bodies, bodies in distress, bodies interacting with each other, and with the natural world. We meet fragmented bodies, a description of a hand, a torso, a collarbone. In his *An Essay Concerning Human Understanding*, John Locke wrote that everyone born into the world is "surrounded by bodies, that perpetually and diversely affect them." In the human world, everyone has a body, and experiences the world, at least in part, from this corporeal vantage point. Poets capitalize on this universal experience to communicate and explain their ideas about the human condition.

Writers' use of the body as subject and the body as metaphor relies on and refers back to common cultural knowledge of the body. For example, during the Enlightenment, "the problem of imaging what was 'out of sight' became critical in the fine arts and the natural sciences" (Stafford, p. xvi). The body and its functions was the unknown, the other, and scholars and artists "invent[ed] metaphors to conjecture about, or embody, the unknown" (p. xvi). Writers referenced popular ideas about the body; for example, during the time that sensibility was in vogue, in Tobias Smollet's *The Expedition of Humphrey Clinker*, a character laments that "everything that discomposes my mind produces a correspondent disorder in my body" (p. 154). Eliza Haywood, who wrote "bodice-ripper" romances, relied heavily on popular knowledge of how sensibility and "the vapours" affected the female body in particular; her texts reference women's blushes, trembles, and sighs as shorthand to indicate sexual desire. In one work, she explains that the heroine dies of a broken heart, an event that was commonly assumed to be possible, given the popular assumption of a strong connection between women's emotional, mental, and physical states.

The advancements in technology and medical science that have occurred since the eighteenth century have worked to create a different, more visual cultural relationship with the human body. Now, the body can readily be "imaged," inside and out, and this imaging has changed popular knowledge about the body. We have wide access to materials about human anatomy (children often start learning about anatomy in elementary school). We have medical technologies of CT and MRI scans that offer visual knowledge of the internal state of the body. Popular culture, such as television shows like *CSI* or *ER*, make constant, often graphic references to the body (usually the injured, sick, or mutilated body) and build storylines around these images, and around bodies that are in peril. Currently, the physical body is not the mysterious unknown that artists or scientists seek to understand. Instead, it is a touchstone, a space of commonality and understanding that artists, particularly poets, can use to explain what still remains unseen: emotional and intellectual experience. Poets use images of the body, or references to corporeal experience, to represent the parts of human experience that remain intangible.

In my own work, bodies occupy a significant amount of space. In the two poems in this anthology I actually use the word "body" or "bodies" by the second line. In "January" I use physical sensation to embody the sound of a voice struggling to speak in and communicate through a foreign language. I work in a medium that allows me to play with language and meter, and I could have attempted to employ words and phrases that might have approximated the sound to which the speaker refers. However, I decided that creating a metaphor based on corporeal experience (though in this case it is the bodies of fish, instead of people, that struggle upstream) would better communicate the feeling of hearing the sound that the speaker experiences. Also, I wanted to draw attention to the physical act of attempting to speak an unfamiliar language, and the social awkwardness that often follows such an attempt.

In my poem "Elizabeth's Monologue: The Metal Mannequin," the body functions as subject, rather than metaphor. As explained in the

poem's footnote, Elizabeth Bathory tortured and killed over 600 serv-
ant girls, and was rumored to have bathed in their blood in the hope
that this ritual would keep her skin youthful looking. Bathory (at least,
the version of Bathory that I have created) was obsessed with her own
physical beauty, and sought to further her own beauty by consuming
that of others. In the poem, she perceives the girl she murders as inferior
because she is Slovakian (Hungarian Bathory was part of the nobility
that then ruled what is now Slovakia); the girl's beauty is not coupled
with social or economic status. Elizabeth occupies, in her world, an all
powerful, dominant position; the girl's body is "cast as deviant and infe-
rior . . . fined in opposition to a norm that is assumed to possess natural
physical superiority" (Thompson, p. 19). Elizabeth, even though she
commits the socially deviant act of murder, rationalizes and normalizes
her behaviour because of her socio-political status, but also because she
believes she possesses a superior status that stems, in part, from her
physical beauty. She claims the authority to mutilate and destroy others'
bodies in order to enhance her own.

"The body" has long been the subject of art, literature, and scien-
tific dialogues, and the use of corporeal images, references, or meta-
phors in poetry is not, in itself, original. However, the possibility exists
for poets (and all writers) to exploit the ubiquity of the body in order
to facilitate the communication of abstract experience, or to investi-
gate political, social, and economic issues. Social and cultural percep-
tions and knowledge of bodies will still shift, expand, and change; so
too will the poetic possibilities for "the body."

WORKS CITED

Locke, John. *An Essay Concerning Human Understanding.* Seventh edition.
London: Printed for J. Churchill and Samuel Manship, 1715-16. Gale
Group: Eighteenth Century Collections Online.

Smollett, Tobias. *The Expedition of Humphrey Clinker.* 1771. New York:
Houghton, 1968.

Stafford, Barbara Maria. *Body Criticism: Imaging the Unseen in Enlightenment
Art and Medicine.* Cambridge, Massachusetts: MIT Press, 1991.

Thompson, Rosemary Garland. "Theorizing Disability." *Extraordinary Bod-
ies: Figuring Physical Disability in American Culture and Literature.* New
York: Columbia UP, 1996. 19-51.

MAMÂHTÂWISIWIN:

TAPPING INTO THE GREAT MYSTERY

I still remember the discussions my father and others would have about the true meaning of Cree words. I myself carried on similar conversations with others as we discussed the layers of meaning in the Cree language. At first, this process of "word defining" led to poetry that was confined to my notebooks and usually through several rewrites. Regrettably, I have long since lost many of these notebooks, but the process that started in the search for meaning in my language is a practice I carry with me.

Central to my poetic process has been the interface between oral and written language. I began to write more poetry at the time the *Crow Hop Café*, a venue for aboriginal writers and performers, was launched in 2000. I found the stage to be a natural setting for my poetry. At its height in 2003, the *Crow Hop* was attracting audiences of 600 people. These oral performances were essential to my process, and I would always shift my poems to fit the folds and the demands of the audience. I also tried to be entertaining, and strived to hold the attention of the crowd. One of the challenges I faced when I published my first book, *Songs to Kill a Wîhtikow*, was to translate the poems from oral performance to the written page. My editor Allan Safarik, was of great assistance in this process.

When I first started writing poetry I saw myself as a performance poet, so I am particularly aware of the rhythms of my poems, their acoustic structure as it were, and I always write with that in mind. I have a bad habit of rewriting my poems moments before I go on stage: especially poems that I have recently written. Often, after a performance I will remember the rhythms that I read, and will edit the poems again, trying to make them as condensed and saturated as possible. I edit out lines that came across as slow, or did not seem central to the narrative I was trying to convey. I always combine the process of writing with reading my poems aloud. As I edit I listen for the economy of the language, word-play, and double meaning and I always try to push the language beyond the ordinary.

My starting point for poetry is the narrative imagination. I try to open a connection between my consciousness and a larger collective memory. The Cree word, *mamâhtâwisiwin*, aptly describes the creative process that I follow — the word could be translated as "tapping into the Great Mystery" or perhaps "tapping into the life-force." It is basically what Old Ben was describing to Luke Skywalker on Tatooine: there is life-force in all things, and as artists and poets, we actively engage it.

The term *ê-mamâhtâwisit*, the verb form of *mamâhtâwisiwin*, means he or she is "spiritually gifted." It could also be translated perhaps as "they know something that you will never know": once I asked how one would translate "funky dancer " in Cree and I was told *ê-mamâhtâwisit*, "she/ he knows something that you will never know" (by the way she dances). Sometimes old Cree words become toys for anthropologists and other cultural tourists, but it should be noted that these terms and ideas have great relevance today. For instance, one Cree term for computer is *"mamâhtâwisi-apâcihican"* which could be rendered as "the powerful machine."

My own poetic process has been heavily intertwined with ancestral memory. While I make no claims of being a traditional storyteller, my work is profoundly grounded in the old stories. I have found great inspiration from these old narratives, and they form the structure through which I make sense of my world, to imagine new characters, and new situations. Because I had the fortune of spending time with my late grandfather, John R. McLeod, I also believe that we have a responsibility to remember, and to hold up old ancestral echoes so future generations will have the same narrative pool from which they can draw inspiration from telling their own stories, in their own time.

My process involves layering language through time and through sound. Like my paintings, I constantly add new layers to my poems, as a response to performances, and oral revisions each layer feeds the next. The process is like a dialogue, a conversation between locations and possibilities. August Rodin spoke of the "living surface" of lines in his work, and I see the acoustic surface of my poems in the same way. The poems, in the moment of creation are spoken performances, are a "living line" of practice embedded with many layers, some older, some deeper, layers being echoed in the present.

In Saskatchewan, there is a rapidly growing Indigenous population, with a large youth population. This young and growing population will need stories for them to make sense of the world around them. The old stories are now being connected to contemporary neechi funk.

Poetry is seen by some as an elitist activity, and distant from the daily lives of many people. However, amongst a growing number young Indigenous people in Saskatchewan, poetry, in all of its forms, is seen as an art form with power that has the ability to tell stories that help people make sense of the world around them. One form is found in the quick wit of hip-hop: dense language, with an underlay of acoustic foundation (beats), full of imagery, and full of rhythm. I see the art of poetry developing further within the large and growing Indigenous population of Saskatchewan, with many trying to bridge old ancestral echoes with the present.

The greatest neechi poets of all were of course the Old Ones, whose memories we carry in our words and bodies. At recent literary event, the Anskohk Aboriginal Literature Award (2005), out of sixteen writers, there were four direct descendents of my grandmother cîhcam (Maria Vandall, née Maria Masaskâpaw). To her spirit and memory, I dedicate all my poems.

THE JAZZ OF POETICS

Writing about poetry and prosody in an attempt to illuminate poetic writing is incredibly difficult. Poetic writing functions at a completely different level than expository writing, and instead attempts to evoke, to explore, and to subtly reveal. There is no illusion or presumption of total understanding, or "knowing" something specifically and completely. Poetic writing is more concerned with relationship, and exploring wonder and mystery. A poem about love does not attempt to quantify love, or to define love categorically — instead a poem evokes love and the human experience, and connects the reader in a relationship with that evoked experience.

In many ways, I don't want to be able to completely describe how I was able to create these poems because I do not want to completely understand the process. I want the mystery to unfold. Having said that, I do believe that analysis can add to the experience of reading a poem.

I have had a great interest in jazz for years — part of my fascination is the fluid structure of the music itself, which is nearly impossible to define completely. Though one can obviously describe chord structures, time signatures, and the concept of improvisation, it still remains difficult to quantify the fluid nature of jazz. I think I was drawn to the lives of jazz musicians for similar reasons. Though I am familiar with their music and much of their stated biographies, much remains mysterious. Poetry became a way to gain some understanding for me.

The three poems included in this anthology come from a larger collection of jazz I have been working on for several years that explores the lives and music of several jazz figures with near-mythic status as cultural forces. I started each of these poems with a central image, which was often visual, and extrapolated from there, improvising like a jazz musician on a chorus structure. The poems occasionally were written quickly, but more often than not, the poems took months, and sometimes years to complete, slowly evolving as I was weaving the content into the form, merging the meaning and the sound into one. The poems built organically in waves, with a loose, open structure, though one that is constantly there, underlying the whole poem. The underlying structure has its own logic and harmonies. The language of poetry is a dance of meaning and sound, entwined like DNA strands, both are needed in order to create life. Sound poetry, though clever and sonically interesting, is often nonsense in terms of content; whereas poetry that strives, often pretentiously, for dense meaning, usually contains no music, rhythm, and when read aloud is like experiencing a slow death.

The Billie Holiday poems both started with sound — and my curiosity of how she could crystallize pain and sadness in songs with a relatively small voice. Both "The Red Dress" and "The Chair" focused on childhood events from Billie Holiday's early life (which may or may not have been true, even though mentioned in biographies). In her case, I was more interested in the emotional truth and the sound of both her music and the resulting poems.

The Duke Ellington poem, "The Cellophane Sky," began as a sound when I first started writing the poem. I had the rhythmic tap of footsteps on a street, in this case an empty, cobble street. From there I built a poem, merging that rhythm with the visual image of Duke sitting alone in the night, listening to that same sound, then tapping out the rhythm on a window ledge, before moving to the piano to start composing a new song. In the poem, that one sound acts as a transition to connect all the aspects of the content.

Jazz becomes an apt and valuable metaphor for writing about poetics because jazz works within and around structure, and the music functions simultaneously both within and without the form. This is probably what makes jazz so difficult to listen to for many people — jazz requires that a listener both hold the song's structure and yet accept the explorations of the musician around that structure — whether defined by rhythm, chord structure, or bar measures.

Jazz is less rigid than, say, classical music, where notes are sequenced in complex patterns, but locked into a permanent structure — jazz moves in fluid waves, conscious of structure, but not completely bound by structure. A jazz musician often takes a structure and then inverts it, bends it, and in doing so, restructures the form — playing with time, space, ambiance, mood. It is like trying to hold water, but magic in that in all its transience, it can be held, if only briefly. A major player like John Coltrane could take a 'popular' structure, like "My Favourite Things", and basically reinvent the meaning of the song, finding new nuances, and, in doing so, creating a new world.

Poets play with language and form in much the same manner — both conscious of the structure and yet often eager to push the limits of that structure in order to contain the music and content of the poem. Each poem creates its own world, with its own structure, its own language, its own inner logic and rules — there can be similarities in form and pattern, but no real duplication. The challenge of each poem is unique unto itself. Ultimately each poem contains its own music, its own rhythm, its own improvised riff and chorus. The narrative drives the music, and the music drives the narrative. An idea gets taken over by the poem's structure, much like a jazz solo — both freed and contained by the chord structure, rhythm, mood, and mode of the song. And when all goes well, and sound and meaning weave together, phonemes and morphemes entwined, a new world is created — the world made flesh, propelled by breath and blood.

Landscape: Rhythm and Light

I've spent much of my life watching and listening, so I hardly noticed when I started calling myself a poet. Looking back, it's easier to see the paths I didn't take. I don't call myself a musician or an artist; but my history in music and art has influenced the poet I've become. At some point in my life, with a decided lack of dedication to practicing piano and a fading interest in colour theory, I found myself writing poetry. Well, that may be stretching the narrative, but it's a beginning.

I took piano lessons for ten years — hated practicing my scales, chords, sight reading. My favourite songs in the Royal Conservatory book for grade eight (my final year) were Chopin's "Sonata in A Minor" and Larysa Kuzmenko's "Mysterious Summer's Night." Both pieces were more about expression and the feeling of the music than the speed of notes and complexity of scales. I could make the notes sing — as though they were words elevated beyond any inadequacies for expression.

I remember walking into a piano lesson and seeing a box of pencil crayons on one of the two baby grands in my teacher's studio. We went through the songs I was working on and chose the colour that I thought best represented the feeling of each piece. That night, I went home and imagined a narrative for those songs. "Sonata in A Minor" would fill the silence of a European cathedral. My teacher had told me that Chopin was obsessed with his fear of being buried alive, so I imagined a funeral for the living — the right hand notes a heartbeat, the left hand melody a mourner's song. "Mysterious Summer's Night" was a conversation between lovers — at times on the very edge of a crescendo, at times intimately *pianissimo*, in the grainy white light of a streetlight in the evening.

I also took art classes. For a while, I wanted to be an artist "when I grew up." There were so many parts of the world I wanted to reflect, to remember. An older cousin, whom I admired greatly and unquestionably when I was young, had a natural talent for sketching and painting. Hanging on the wall of their home was a pencil sketched portrait she had made of our Oma and Opa (our grandparents), Dutch immigrants who died when we were all still quite young. My uncle was so proud of that portrait, which my cousin had copied from a professionally taken photograph. Much like the photographer, she had captured the living and dying, the memory and strangeness of the image. But, more than that, there was a love — a mourning — in her pencil strokes, so dark in places the lead reflected light off the page.

I never did try to sketch or paint the image of my grandparents. I wasn't sure I could. But I wrote a couple short stories about them over the years and, eventually, a poem or two. They are the portraits I've made, the images of memory.

After I graduated from university, I took a Monday night painting class at the local community arts centre. I hesitated to take the class at first, concerned that it would become another interruption to any time I might find to write, but the class taught me more than just techniques for painting with acrylic. It helped me to understand how my interest in art has contributed to my poetry. Sitting in front of my blank canvas, I would wish I could use words instead of paint.

My art instructor often spoke of Monet, whom he considers to be one of the world's great artists. He told us that impressionism is about more than reflecting the things you see — it's about trying to understand them. It's about forms, colours, tones, light. Monet would take his canvas into a field, his garden at Giverny, or onto the sidewalk in front of the Rouen Cathedral. He would paint until the certain angle of light he wanted fell or disappeared. On canvas, his impressions of that light are more than just visual — they become a mood, a perception, a rhythm of breath or brushstrokes. They make me think that life is lived in the ephemeral, that poems are the quick notes I take. Poems are a reflection of how that certain light falls on my world and the feeling I'm left with.

I grew up in a town just off the Trans Canada, in a landscape defined by its horizon. The landscape, the horizon line, became a part of me. Much of my life was spent meditating on the land and sky, on the stretch of highway between my town and the city. Every day I saw a different sky, a different geography. From a young age I knew that the shadows in the snow-covered fields weren't grey (the pencil crayon colour everyone used for shadows), they were blue. A cloud over a field in the summer turned the bleached grain fields brown. For me, the landscape is a feeling and a kind of knowing. It exists in relationship to me and I to it. The light and air — the lyric and narrative — move around me and through me.

Monet once said, "For me, a landscape does not exist in its own right, since its appearance changes at every moment; but the surrounding atmosphere brings it to life — the light and the air which vary continually. For me, it is only the surrounding atmosphere which gives subjects their true value." My poems are rhythm and light, the intertwining of music, art, and life.

THE LONG POEM:

WRITING THE NEVER-ENDING

I see the long poem as a reaching back, a longing inside each moment, slippage, an attempt to record and recover, as exhaustibly as possible, that which is unrecordable and unrecoverable. My grandmother's memory in the early stages of dementia. Ancestral stories buried in an aspen forest. What is lost in the reaching out. Leaves dying off into a new season, "light shriveling forward". It's the paradoxical walk towards memory. Learning to return "to a place you have never been".

It's also a recording of process. The meandering and the wandering it takes to write. I've come to accept that my particular writing process is slow. It takes me a long time to figure out what I'm writing about and when I do, where I'm going with it. It's in the writing that I find my way. The long poem is a record of that discovery. The long poem opens up the writing for me. Gives me the freedom to discover — allows me to walk openly and attentively toward "a point of no light". Shorter, discrete poems have always been difficult for me in that I don't think in this way. Each short poem I write always opens up to the next, so it feels much more natural and exciting for me to just continue to write in a sequence of fragments. Writing has become much like a long walk with my three-year-old daughter — I have learned to accept we may never get to the park! I feel toddler-legged myself as a writer. I have to let go of my intention in order to truly discover. The long poem is my slow, curious walk. Here I can let go of destination and play for a while. It's the illusion, if nothing else, of freedom, "a broken cattle fence that says *runrun*," a boundless space opening up to words.

What holds the long poem together, for me, is its insistent circling. The lyrical way it walks around and around a subject and then reaches out with the curious hands of language. It's writing the infinite space between where we are now and what we can remember, between root and drifting seed. In this space the long poem can become unwieldy, overgrown, clumsy and tangled. As Lyn Hejinian writes in her book-length poem *My Life* "[w]hat follows a strict chronology has no memory." The long poem I am trying to write progresses in its digressions. I begin meditating on leaves for instance, and it is really about birth, not just the imminent birth of my daughter, but the birth of generations before me, about my grandmother and her grandmother and how this is all part of the future. It's not just a remembering, but a meditation on memory, about belonging to what is behind us. The long poem reaches back as far as it can. Like a child, it wants to go too far. Over and over it longs for what cannot be described or remembered. Like the growth rings of a tree, it circles itself as it reaches, it writes around.

The long poem is also a digging. The heels familiarizing themselves on the path, the heart circling down. It's those roots underfoot, all connected as they reach out. "Trembling Aspen" was written on a series of walks through aspen forests in northern Saskatchewan. One of the forests is located at the historic site of Fort aux Trembles, an 18th century trading post also known as Isaac's House after my 9th generation grandfather, Isaac Batt. It is believed one of his children was stillborn and is buried there. The long poem is my archeological dig, the present reaching back into a "land . . . that will forget . . . its child graves". The extended poem remembers the extended family. It is a searching. A long walk through the woods of memory. It allows for a flow of narrative, the incorporation of multiple voices, and ultimately supports the nature of my research: to trace the long lines of ancestry and the stories that unfold within this history, stories that clarify my own place in the world, that illuminate — like a "map / of roots when you hold me to the light" — the context of my belonging.

During the writing of "Trembling Aspen" I worked with a great mentor, Don Domanski, who recognized my constant dissatisfaction in my work as a natural part of writing poetry because, as he so profoundly articulated, "the poem always fails." In writing the long poem I am avoiding the eventual failing that is the poem. I am going as far as possible to say what I will never be able to say, I am reaching out to "that which never ends".

It's the possibility of this "never-ending" that draws me to the long poem. The form represents movement, that which is cyclical. It leaps. Trembles. Gestures to the connectedness of the world "as if sky plus sun must make leaves" (Hejinian). In "Trembling Aspen", not only does the poem write away from an end, but its ending is just another opening, "a little gold door / you wait to enter." I see the long poem as a way to write along a curve. The poem as part of a bigger whole. It is something I follow on a slope, like a divining rod, pulled to hidden currents. I write poetry because of the way it opens up the world, because of the possibilities at each turn. In writing the long poem I give myself the freedom of never ending. I walk with possibility in front of me, toward the next turn in the path, and then the next.

WORK CITED

Hejinian, Lyn. My Life. Los Angeles: Sun & Moon Press, 1987.

STREETCAR OUT, OWL'S CLAW IN:

SOME NOTES ON LYRIC POETRY

1. Poets try to articulate the blind universe that passes through everyone.

2. A great poet who was born in Saskatchewan, Eli Mandel, confided to me that once he'd completed a poem, he never knew if he would ever be a poet again. This made no sense to me at the time: I was twenty-two, had just bought him a glass of his favourite red wine, had been trying to read some of the many books he'd spoken about, and I thought, then, that writing poetry meant hard work, sure, but that for someone like Eli, being a poet was a complex, yet basic vocation, something continuous, something that he simply did — brilliantly. And I wanted to be like him. It's been about twenty-five years since we had that conversation, and one of the griefs in my life is that I can't talk to him now. I was smart enough to recognize the range of Eli's generosity, but I was too young to understand hardly anything of his terror, his joy, and his endless humility. I don't presume to have any knowledge about how Eli felt when he wrote a poem, but I do know that when I'm trying to write — and I spend far more time trying to write than succeeding — there's a small cluster of faces, a few lines from a few poems, varying colours and geographical places flickering just off to the left of my vision, and Eli's presence, there to my left, is something of which I'm constantly aware.

3. Obsessed with transience, lyric poems unwrap immediacy with undiscovered combinations of words. They rebel against time and the daily blur of what happens. A lyric poem is a kind of reaching out in the attempt to nail something down, to claim something that can, finally, be ours. While poems probe and often celebrate the nature of the present — the present, that amazing glue to which nothing sticks — they often manifest a radical skepticism. Lyric poems accentuate how little we know about experience and how scarcely we understand words themselves. And at the end of the day, we own so little, almost nothing at all.

4. Put differently, lyric poetry enacts the war between what's visible and the amplitude of what's missing.

5. Dylan Thomas's "Fern Hill" was the first piece of literature that spoke to me. I was in high school. When the teacher read the lines describing horses, and Adam experiencing the first light, something went off in me. I had to leave, so went to the window and jumped out (not a heroic feat, the class room was on the first floor) and walked back to town, closed myself in my room, and reread, reread and reread Thomas's lines. It would be partially true to say that every poem I've written has been the attempt to recover that original astonishment at what words can do and how rich the world can be made to seem. I say "partially true" because, on the one hand, lyric poems may be consistent, though sporadic, love letters addressed both to other poems and the world, but, on the other hand, they can also be jeremiads, often anguished repudiations of not only whatever the world is but also the limitations of what words can say.

6. Poems speak to other poems, certainly, but more important, they try to seize the actual, phenomenal world, try to splinter off bits of reality, which is always newly happening. A poem's power depends upon a curious tension: it must reflect the world in an honest and original way and simultaneously it must articulate something that the world, until then, has never contained. A poem is successful if it invents an exacting voice. But this voice doesn't belong to the writer. Lyric poetry has almost nothing to do with self-expression. Working

on a draft, you sense an implicit shape, a beginning rhythm in the words that desires fruition. At this point, the poem takes over and you stop trying to say anything in particular at all. You merely listen.

7. I find composition to be completely baffling. It took a year and a half to round out "The Colour White" and maybe four hours for "Birds, Pity Nostradamus." Regardless of the time it takes to write a poem, the images that show up engage a net of slow drift. The Nostradamus poem, a kind of ghazal, started with a Tabloid newspaper article I'd seen that day in a grocery store. When I began writing I'd no idea that the poem would end, an afternoon later, recalling a woman I loved who killed herself in the mid 1980s. Reading the completed poem, I recognize that the final line became almost inevitable once the first line was jotted down. During composition the mind may open itself to seemingly abandoned memories and perceptions, but that doesn't mean a poem simply charts this interior process. There's an image that initially was part of "The Colour White": an overturned streetcar on a small city street. I didn't know where this image came from; it just popped into my head. The streetcar strongly insisted on being in the poem, persisted through several drafts, but I eventually cut it because it seemed too idiosyncratic, too narrowly personal (though I've never seen a streetcar lying on its side). I finished the poem, left out the streetcar and went on to other things. But a few weeks ago there was a photo in *The Globe and Mail* commemorating the 1956 revolution in Hungary — and there was that precise overturned streetcar. I wasn't alive in 1956 to see the original news image, so I must have encountered it later as a child. I remembered none of these historical details when I originally worked on the poem. The image simply presented itself, and then the exigencies of the poem that wanted to be written took over: streetcar out, owl's claw in. But I like to think that somewhere, hovering just beyond or beneath the page, is an homage to the exact defiance that caused people to riot in Budapest in 1956.

ON THE GENESIS OF "MESNER'S DEAD"

I knew Dahlia before I met Mesner. We worked together five nights a week (Tuesday to Saturday) at Bugsy's Bar and Grill during the summer of 1997. This was back in Moose Jaw, a year after we finished high school. We became close friends working in such close quarters (Bugsy's is about the length of the number of cigarettes you could smoke in an hour lined up end-to-end) and I got to know her pretty good. Dahlia was seeing someone at the time so things never got too far, but even after she moved with this guy to Calgary we kept in touch.

Dahlia started dancing (by which I mean stripping or peeling, not plain, old "grab your partner and spin 'em 'round" dancing) a few months after that relationship ended; and, I suspect, her wanting to dance had something to do with the break-up. Every time we talked about it on the phone she made the same joke: "The money's too good to pass up; and my skills are too good to waste." She'd done a dance or two for some birthday boys at Bugsy's (and, come to think of it, for a few birthday girls, as well) so I couldn't really argue. On her way to shows out east, or on her way back through to Calgary, she would visit me in Regina. I was at university then but still bartending nights. More than once while watching me work ("a nice change of roles," she joked), she said that I was the steadiest guy she had. I never once had the guts to say that she was the only human thing I had going, too.

Things got bad for Dahlia after her older sister died in a car accident. That was in 2001. The car her sister had been travelling in was sideswiped in Saskatoon. The roads had been icy but the guy who'd hit her had been drunk. I met up with Dahlia in Saskatoon for the funeral, and then stayed with her in Calgary for as long as I could. I eventually took off for Taiwan to teach. I invited Dahlia but she said she really wanted to just keep dancing, though her circles got smaller and smaller as she travelled less, sticking mostly with the Alberta circuit. The driver who killed her sister received the full ten years.

When I returned to Canada in late 2003 is when I met Mesner. He had joined Dahlia's support group, for the relatives and friends of the victims of drunk drivers, after leaving BC in search of work. I'd gotten home from overseas empty-handed, and still pretty well empty-headed, and I didn't think much of Mesner one way or the other. He was about ten years older than us, hardworking; quiet, but a nice enough guy. He supported Dahlia's dancing, and her extended mourning, and I was just happy that he let me crash with him (the place Dahlia rented with her diminished income was too small for two) while I got back on my feet.

A few months into my stay, while waiting to take off for work, the television gave Mesner away. I was watching one of those local, low-budget human interest shows (with "movie-of-the-week" levels of the maudlin). The episode was about a surgeon who prevented severe scarring on children injured in wild animal attacks (maybe that's not quite right, but you get the idea). During a "Dr.-interacting-sensitively-with-recovering-patient" moment, I saw, in a bed in the background, a guy who looked just like Mesner, except he had a thick gash running from his forehead to his chin. The same program ran on the same station twelve hours later (thank God for local content requirements) and after the second time around I knew it was Mesner. I had to investigate.

What I learned, following a ton of phone calls and two trips to Saskatoon, is that Mesner had been in the backseat of the car that killed Dahlia's sister. Drunk, he'd gotten pretty messed-up himself, supposedly shooting through the front windshield. Most sources testified to this, while a few said he'd thrown himself out the backdoor as the car slid across the icy street, though I could never officially confirm either story. The receptionists at the clinic wouldn't give me anything, and the administration was even less cooperative. A guy in supplies, who'd happened to hear about me, said he'd been in AA with Mesner following the accident (yeah, Mesner really had a thing for support groups). Pretty much everything Mesner had told Dahlia — about being from BC, about losing his mom — was bullshit. But why did he lie? And why did he come looking for her?

I started some poems around that time, as a way of working some of this stuff out, but I kept them to myself. I wanted to tell Dahlia the truth, but what truth? That Mesner had been in the car? That he saw her sister die? That he was responsible for . . . what? Was it even my place to tell? Before I could get anything out of Mesner, he left. He knew that I knew. I kept track of him for a bit, for her, following him from Calgary to Winnipeg to Thunder Bay, and then sweeping through Quebec as he made his way to Nova Scotia. Twice I came to his apartment door, but I never knocked; and whenever I called him I never made it past his first word ("hello") before hanging up.

On March 12, 2005, I stood with Dahlia's parents as they buried their youngest daughter beside their oldest. Alcohol was involved again, but no cars — just a little vomit and a body, motionless, on its back. I've done my best in the months since to make sense of what happened, trying to find the right form. What would convey this mess of deception and reflection? What would clarify its blurred impermanence? What survives in what remains? These pictures in my head I can't let go. Though I guess it's finally okay to share what I've written, I've changed all the names to protect those involved.

On the Genesis of "On the Genesis of 'Mesner's Dead'"

Mesner's Response:

I would like to begin in the spirit of the "will to confess" that seems to haunt Daniel's poem, a will that takes the form of everything from all those support groups to my own dealings with Dahlia: "His name is Daniel Tysdal. And 'Mesner's Dead' is made up, a lie." There never was a Dahlia who Daniel's fictional surrogate mourned. There was never a deceased sister. There was never even a "me," Mesner, who held a hand in the events surrounding each woman's respective demise.

Any of you who know Daniel can probably appreciate the detours and dead ends I ran up against when I called him and tried to get an answer to the simple question, why? Why start the poems by telling the story the poems already told? And why make it a true, personal account, one that "really happened"? In the end, Daniel grew frustrated with my inquiries and hung up.

Daniel's Interjection:

The answer to Mesner's questions, an answer I repeated throughout our conversation but that he refused to accept, is simple: clarity.

By introducing the poems with the story of Mesner and Dahlia, I brought into relief the narrative events, character motivations and thematic concerns that are present in the poems, but buried and blurred rather than explicitly stated. The preface is a kind of dumb show or chorus; it lays out the ways of its players, while stating overtly the piece's fundamental fascination with how questions of personal and artistic responsibility are shaped by not only the contingency of disaster (i.e., the car crash) but the disaster of this very contingency (i.e., the crisis of representation that sustains Mesner's deception, Dahlia's extended mourning and my own infinite regressive pursuit).

Similarly, the "as if real" slant of the introduction clarifies the reader's position; it is a mode of narrative solicitation and seduction that, at once traditional and contemporary, welcomes the reader in. Nodding in the direction of the history of literary eye-witness accounts, the "as if real" conceit also heeds the popular reverence for revelation through "the real thing," a reverence demonstrated in cultural happenings as diverse as CSI's aestheticization of positivism; Michael Moore's docu-tainments; the uproar over James Frey; and the blogsphere's popularization of the public personal diary.

Mesner's Response:

Clarity. Right. Uh-huh. The "as if real." I see.

But I'm pretty sure the whole "On the Genesis of Mesner"-thing is more than crib notes or a friendly, "how you doing?"

Despite Daniel's best efforts to keep them concealed, I've seen the early drafts of "Mesner's Dead." And it's something to see how much the poem changed. A personal look at regret and addiction, complete with a very "un-Tysdal" speaking (at once confessional and concise), morphed into a meditation on a good friend's attempt to work through the "here and now" endurance of "there and then" sins. It wasn't until he had written about these more personal experiences that Daniel's made-up trinity appeared: the Mesner, the Dahl and the li'l sis. The motifs of distortion soon followed, the formal quirks, and, finally, the lie: that we were real. That we moved among you. And he knew us.

The "I was there" preface was his way of sneaking back into the picture without having to disclose anything of himself. The coward's oldest trick: don't just build the mask, but the puppet who will wear it.

Daniel's Interjection:

The poems were, admittedly, very confessional to begin with, but "On the Genesis of 'Mesner's Dead'" was there from the start as well, haunting the project's horizon and drawing it toward a different kind of "personal." All along the poems wanted to stop simply floundering in the single story of obsession and addiction, of guilt and regret, and start telling the story of the story that allows this telling to take place. Not "speaking to the tribe" exactly, but wondering: how does the tribe try to speak the suffering of one?

That's why the narrative I worked with ended up being such a cliché. It's a movie-of-the-week melodrama with a public service announcement drizzled around the edges. The compulsory drama of confession is handed over to the loveable drunk and the stripper with a heart of gold. What I ended up with, however accidentally, is a kind of mock-epic, though not in the traditional sense of the term. This is not a minor happening told in the lofty tones and soaring language of the epic mode. This is the present's primetime incarnation of the epic couched in a minor language, a language that, from the perspective of the popular, is invisible.

Mesner's Response:

I get it. "On the Genesis of 'Mesner's Dead'" distils a myth. The poems are one incarnation. Dahlia's sister is the swan. Me and Dahlia are Leda. And now any writer can have a go at struggling with our struggling with our dim impregnation. Our silence. For the sake of my sanity, I hope not.

And for the sake of your soul, I hope one day you'll be able to admit that some of the loss here is your responsibility. Some of the failure, too.

Mesner's Interjection:

Daniel brought me a story about my story, half of it written in my voice and half of it written in his.

I said, "It's a lie."

He said, "I know."

Daniel's Response

and I'm sticking to it.

Sheri Benning' poetry and fiction have been published in *PRISM International, Prairie Fire, The Malahat Review, Grain, Event, The Fiddlehead* and other magazines. Her first book of poetry, *Earth After Rain* (2001) was a recipient of two Saskatchewan Book Awards. Her poetry has also appeared in the anthologies *Breathing Fire 2* and *Listening with the Ear of the Heart.* In spring 2004 she was awarded a Saskatchewan Lieutenant Governor's Award for the Arts (artists under 30 years of age). Her second collection of poetry is forthcoming from Brick Books in fall 2007.

Belinda Betker is a full-time health care worker. She is a founding member of the Saskatoon-based writing group *Sisters' Ink*, which has collectively published a chapbook, *Where Dragonflies Go* (2005). Belinda is a creative writing instructor for City of Sask-atoon Leisure Services, and she has been a board member of the Saskatoon Writers Coop and the Saskatchewan Writers Guild.

Beverley Brenna has published four books for children, the most recent being *Wild Orchid*, a YA novel from Red Deer Press. Her poetry has appeared in magazines such as *Grain* and *Dandelion*, and she has had poetry and short fiction broadcast on CBC Radio. She lives on an acreage near Saskatoon with her husband and three sons, and works as a special education teacher.

Carla Braidek has lived in the boreal forest near Big River, Saskatchewan for over 25 years. She and her partner, Garry, have raised five children and numerous horses. They are now raising tree seedlings for reforestation. In 2003 Carla released her chapbook *Quickening* with B-) Print Editions. Thistledown Press published her first book, *Carrying the Sun* in April, 2005. It was shortlisted for the Poetry Award at the 2005 Saskatchewan Book Awards.

Lynn Cecil is a writer and artist whose poems are often inspired by her oil paintings. She lives in Regina with her husband and two children, and enjoys traveling and scuba diving. Second Story Press recently released *Outside of Ordinary: Women's Travel Stories*, which she co-edited.

Sandy Easterbrook has lived 26 years in Saskatoon, where she works as an art conservator, specializing in the restoration of paintings. She and her partner are in the process of relocating to the land of milk and honey, where they will live in a straw bale house, raise sheep and bees, and produce artisanal cheese. Her poetry has appeared in *Spring* and *Transition*.

Bernice Friesen's fiction, poetry, and visual art has been in and on the covers of many books and periodicals. The title story of her book of short fiction, *The Seasons Are Horses* (1995), won the 1996 Vicky Metcalf Short Story Award. *Sex, Death, and Naked Men*, a collection of poetry, was published by Coteau Books in 1998. She lives in Saskatoon with her husband, son, and daughter.

Tracy Hamon is a Regina writer whose work has been published in numerous periodicals. In 2005 she published her first book of poetry, *This is Not Eden*, which was a finalist for two Saskatchewan Book Awards. Hamon was the 2005 recipient of the City of Regina Writing Award.

Julia Herperger lives in Saskatoon. Her work has been published in journals such as *Arc*, *Grain*, and *Room of One's Own*, and was also included in the anthology *Listening with the Ear of the Heart* (2003). She has also had work broadcast on CBC Radio's *Gallery*.

Wanda Hurren is a Saskatchewan poet/photographer who writes "snapshots" of everyday life, with a focus on notions of place and identity. Her poetry has been published in *Gender, Place and Culture: A Journal of Feminist Geography*, *Canadian Women's Studies*, and the *Canadian Journal of Prairie Literature*. She lives in Regina.

Taylor Rae Leedahl is a student at the University of Saskatchewan. Her main areas of interest are studio art, art history, and English. Taylor began writing and reading at a young age. She has been published in *WindScript* and *Claremont Review*, and was a competitor in the 2006 CBC National Poetry Face-Off. She lives in Saskatoon.

Laura Edna Lacey is originally from Southern Ontario, although Saskatoon has been her home base for the past ten years. She has also spent time in Indonesia, Guatemala, India, and Sled Lake, Saskatchewan. She earned a BA Honours in English at the University of Saskatchewan, and has given public readings of her poetry in Saskatchewan, Ontario, the US and India. She has published her work in *Room of One's Own* and in the chapbook, *Alongside Silence.*

Anne Lazurko, a mother of four, lives, farms, and writes poetry and fiction near Weyburn. She completed the Humber Correspondence Course in July 2006, and is a member of the Weyburn Writers Group and the BEES in Regina. In 2004 she was an apprentice in the SWG mentorship program.

Holly Luhning is the author of *Sway* (2003), a book of poetry which was shortlisted for a 2004 Saskatchewan Book Award. Her work has appeared in various Canadian journals and anthologies. In 2005 Luhning was awarded the "30 Below" Lieutenant Governors Arts Award to recognize young artists. In 2006 she won CBC's regional Poetry Face-Off, and represented Saskatchewan in the national competition.

Sharon MacFarlane has published a short story collection, *Driving off the Map*. She has had stories broadcast on CBC Radio, and an excerpt from one of her stories was read at the Seasonal Gala at Government House in Regina in December, 2005. She lives with her husband on a farm near Beechy, Saskatchewan.

Neal McLeod is an accomplished visual artist whose paintings have been exhibited across Canada. He is well known as a humorist with the comedy group, The Bionic Bannock Boys, and a maker of underground films. His first collection of poetry, *Songs to Kill a Wihtikow,* was a finalist in three categories at the 2005 Saskatchewan Book Awards, including Book of the Year. In 2006 *Songs to Kill a Wihtikow* was a finalist for the McNally Robinson Aboriginal Book of the Year Award and was the recipient of the national Aboriginal Poetry Award. In 2006 McLeod moved to Peterborough, Ontario to teach in the Aboriginal Studies Program at Trent University.

Wynne Nicholson is a poet and registered massage therapist who lives in Saskatoon. She won the W. O. Mitchell Bursary and the Gertrude Story Scholarship in 1994. Her fist book, *Small Gifts,* was published in 2005 and was a finalist in poetry at the Saskatchewan Book Awards. Her poems have appeared in *Grain, Vintage,* and *FreeLance.*

Brenda Niskala is a poet and fiction writer who has been a cultural industries executive director, a crisis counselor, a legal aid lawyer, a writer in residence, and a branch representative for ACTRA. She has two chapbooks, *What Butterflies do at Night* (2005) and *Emma's Horizon* (2000), one co-authored collection, *Open 24 Hours* (1997), and a book of poetry, *Ambergris Moon* (1983). She has been published in numerous anthologies, including *Listening with the Ear of the Heart, Loadstone, Sky High, Dancing Visions, Heading out, Bridges 4, What is Already Known,* and numerous magazines.

Jeff Park is a writer from Saskatoon, currently employed in the College of Education, University of Saskatchewan. He works in a variety of *genres,* including short fiction, poetry, and playwriting. He recently published a book on writing theory, entitled *Writing at the Edge: Narrative and Writing Process Theory,* which was released by Peter Lang Press in New York in 2005.

Dolores Reimer lives with her family in Dundurn, Saskatchewan, from where she has directed her various activities as a writer, quilter, literary press publicist, and bookstore event co-ordinator. She has published a novella, *Ladies & Escorts,* and a collection of poetry, *Stone Baby,* which was a finalist at the 2004 Saskatchewan Book Awards. An active and intrepid genealogist, Reimer's next book of poetry will follow the genealogical trail of her family history.

Paula Jane Remlinger recently completed an MA in English at the University of Saskatchewan on the poetry of Saskatchewan writer John V. Hicks. She has been previously published in *In Medias Res* and *Backyard Ashes,* and is also the author of two teacher resource guides from Thistledown Press. She lives in Saskatoon.

Mansel Robinson is a Saskatoon-based playwright. His work includes *Colonial Tongues, Collateral Damage, The Heart As It Lived, Downsizing Democracy, Spitting Slag, Ghost Trains, Street Wheat, Scorched Ice,* and *Picking Up Chekhov.* He has been writer-in-residence at the Pierre Berton House in Dawson City, Yukon, Northern Light Theatre, Edmonton, the University of Windsor and, most recently, at the Regina Public Library. His most recent play, *Bite the Hand,* was presented as a staged reading at the Saskatchewan Playwrights Centre's 2005 Spring Festival of New Plays.

Crystal Sikma is a Regina-based writer. She has an honours degree in English from the University of Regina, with a women's studies minor and a specialization in creative writing. She has attended the Sage Hill Writing Experience twice, and was an apprentice in the 2006 Saskatchewan Writers Guild mentorship program with Judith Krause. Her poems have been published in *In Medias Res.*

Jennifer Still's poetry has appeared in many Canadian journals, including *The Fiddlehead, Prairie Fire, CV2, The New Quarterly,* and *Descant,* and has also been broadcast on CBC Radio. She lives in Saskatoon with her husband, son, and daughter, where she is co-founder of JackPine Press. *Saltations,* her first book of poetry, was published in 2005 by Thistledown Press and was a finalist in three categories at the 2006 Saskachewan Book Awards. "Trembling Aspen" is from her current manuscript in progress.

Michael Trussler teaches English at the University of Regina. He has published poetry, short fiction, and literary criticism. A number of his poems and stories have won prizes. Trussler is an editor with *Wascana Review,* published out of the University of Regina. His first collection of stories, *Encounters,* released by NeWest Press, was the recipient of the City of Regina Book Award and the Saskatchewan Book of the Year Award at the 2006 Saskatchewan Book Awards. In the fall of 2007, Hagios Press will publish Trussler's first collection of poetry, *Accidental Animals.*

Daniel Scott Tysdal received the John V. Hicks Manuscript Award from the Saskatchewan Writers Guild for *Predicting the Next Big Advertising Breakthrough Using a Potentially Dangerous Method,* which was subsequently published in 2006 by Coteau Books. It was nominated for the First Book Award and was the recipient of the Anne Szumigalski Poetry Award at the 2006 Saskatchewan Book Awards. Tysdal's poetry has appeared in a number of Canadian literary journals and has aired on CBC Radio, where he was a finalist in the 2005 National Poetry Face-Off. A poem from this collection, "An Experiment in Form," received an honourable mention at the National Magazine Awards. Born in Moose Jaw, Tysdal is completing his master's degree in English and has worked as a bartender, groundskeeper, and English teacher. He continues to live in Moose Jaw.

Joanne Weber lives in Regina where she is employed with the school board and teaches in the Deaf and Hard of Hearing program at Thom Collegiate. She has studied philosophy, theology, English literature, and history emerging with a BA Honours in English literature, with a minor in philosophy. A master's in library science soon followed, as well as BEd and a year of graduate work in deaf education. Weber is fluent in American Sign Language and has taken leadership roles in the deaf community at the local, provincial and national levels. She lectures at SIAST, the University of Regina, and the University of Saskatchewan in deaf education. She has published poems in several journals across Canada. Her first book of poetry, *The Pear Orchard*, will appear in 2007 from Hagios Press.

Barbara Klar was born in Saskatoon. Her first book of poems, *The Night You Called Me a Shadow*, was co-winner of the 1993 Gerald Lampert Award. She has also published *The Blue Field* (1999), and the chapbook, *Tower Road* (2004). Her third full-length collection, *Cypress*, will appear from Brick Books in 2008. Klar has worked as a tree planter, bush cook, editor, mentor, and freelance writer for both print and radio. She lives with her partner and her deerhound in a farmyard northwest of Saskatoon.

Paul Wilson was born in Lacombe, Alberta in 1954. He is a poet, publisher, editor, and cultural worker. He has worked both as a writer and closely with writers for over 25 years in Saskatchewan. In December 2006 he published a chapbook, *When Seeing Fails,* with Saskatoon's JackPine Press. He is the author of three books of poetry, including *The Long Landscape* (1999), which won the City of Regina Book Award. In 2007 Wolsak & Wynn Publishers will publish his fourth collection, *Turning Mountain*. He works as Member Services & Outreach Manager at Nature Saskatchewan, and lives in Regina with his wife, Elizabeth George, and their daughters, Emily and Sarah.